THE DYSFUNCTIONAL LEADER

THE PATHOLOGY OF FLAWED LEADERSHIP

Todd Marshall Hearnsberger

A Publication of Strategic Organizational Solutions

Todd Marshall Hearnsberger
c: 817.505.5663
e: strategicorgsolutions@gmail.com

The Dysfunctional Leader

By Todd Marshall Hearnsberger

Table of Contents

Dedications

First and foremost, this book would have never been written unless by the prompting of the Holy Spirit. It is because of Jesus and His never-ending dedication to us as His children do I offer my deepest gratitude for allowing me to serve in His kingdom for such a time as this and write this book for His glory.

To my better half, Stephanie, who has been my rock and unwavering support during the writing of this book. Your steadfast love, encouragement, and sacrifices made this book possible. Thank you for believing in me even when I doubted myself. I am blessed beyond measure to share this journey with you.

To my incredible offspring, Hannah and Grafton, who bring immeasurable joy and purpose to our lives. Watching you both grow into the incredible young adults you are has been my life's greatest privilege. May you always lead with integrity, compassion, and courage. Know that you are deeply loved and that I am forever proud of you both.

Introduction

In my decades studying leadership and serving as a leader, I have found dysfunctional leaders tragically common, though no less painful for their common occurrence. Even though we see it often, the immense damage that dysfunctional leaders cause in organizations remains tragic and inexcusable. What distinguishes functional leaders from dysfunctional leaders is not impossible perfection but their humility to identify flawsand commitment to managing toxicity for the greater good. Even well-intentioned organizations can promote or tolerate dysfunctional leaders for shortsighted economic or political reasons.

My aim for this book is to help leaders honestly assess when they have become dysfunctional influences, whether intentionally or not. The journey back is long, but possible if the change is desired strongly enough. By examining "how the mighty fall," as Jim Collins wrote, leaders gain perspective on their true place within organizations and society. Our charge is leadership, empowering others in pursuit of extraordinary goals, not raw dominance imposing our ego on the world.

Recent headlines blare larger-than-life stories of well-intentioned leadership gone horribly awry. Theranos founder Elizabeth Holmes, once Silicon Valley's darling, faces years in prison for massive investor fraud enabled by her draconian leadership style. Activision Blizzard's CEO Bobby Kotick oversaw a pervasive culture of sexual harassment stemming from the top. Boeing executives ignored clear safety concerns, leading to horrific crashes that took hundreds of innocent lives.

The sobering truth is that there's no shortage of unprincipled, incompetent and authoritarian leadership contaminating the highest levels of organizations today. This book will dive deep into what causes such dysfunction to rear its ugly head and guide readers in spotting the red flags early before real damage is done.

While there is dark humor to be found in the absurd extremes of bad leadership, the real-world impacts on employees and organizations are no laughing matter. The costs to mental health, self-esteem, productivity, culture and long-term performance can be severe when narcissists, bullies and tyrants reign. This book aims to entertain but also equip readers with an understanding of how to deal with dysfunctional leaders and heal contaminated environments. Arm yourself with knowledge so that you aren't a poor gazelle left quivering when your lion of a boss is on the warpath.

I do not want to portray myself as the messiah of all things leadership. In fact, I've had my fair share of stumbles and dysfunctional moments as a leader over the years. Looking back, I see the mistakes I've made as a leader and wish I could go back and fix the times when I acted dysfunctionally. While I have made my own leadership mistakes, my occasional stumbles pale in comparison to the severe dysfunction I've directly experienced from toxic workplaces and leaders over my career. I have also heard far too many horrific stories from others scarred by abusive and incompetent leadership. I have decided to save some dysfunctional leader's reputations by not tellingmy side of the story. It is best to stay silent as possible throughthe storms. I have come to realize that bad people usually destroy themselves in the process of trying to destroy you.

The best leaders I know are students of leadership. There is no such thing as an expert leader. It does not exist. There is no such thing as an expert parent. It does not exist. Functional leaders are to be students of leadership. Even the most senior leaders are constantly reading books, reading articles, watching videos, and having conversations about becoming better leaders. They are always in learning mode. I believe that anyone who wants to be a functional leader must choose to be a student of the subject. Like anything, if you want to be good at something, you have to study it.

Each of my personal experiences with dysfunctional leaders taught me unforgettable lessons about ineffective leadership styles and their impacts. However, witnessing their dysfunctions up close gave me a passion for helping leaders avoid similar pitfalls. By understanding that we all make mistakes, we can learn how to help each other recover when failures happen.

In the following pages, with piercing observations, we will dissect the hallmarks of some of the worst types of leaders and dysfunctional organizational cultures. The bully who berates and manipulates. Incompetent leaders messing up basic duties. The ethical transgressor playing by their own crooked rules. The narcissist obsessed with status and power over people. We'll meet them all.

While this book looks at dysfunctional leaders, it also shows how to improve the organizational culture when toxicity sets in. There is still hope for positive change if dysfunctional behavior is faced honestly and with a commitment to improving. When we understand that we also have flaws, we stop criticizing others and instead, help them and ourselves improve. My goal is not to punish dysfunctional leaders, but to show the way forward so we can move positively into the future. Leaders falter, and cultures corrode. But they need not fail. The same self-awareness needed to be a functional leader can also help dysfunctional leaders improve, if they are willing to listen. However, people must give honest feedback, and dysfunctional leaders need to listen to it.

On these pages, we'll explore stories of folly and corruption that make headlines. But also whispers of stories that never get into the mainstream spotlight. If you feel trapped in dysfunction, take heart. Others have escaped its gravity well, and so can you. If you seek to lead well, take heed. Any of us can become the oppressor rather than the liberator. But by learning from past falls, with care and moral courage, we can write new futures. For too long, we have tolerated the dysfunctions of unfit leaders who are undeserving of such an honorable title. But now, it's time to expose them for who they really are at their core.

Let the journey of knowledge and lessons learned begin...

Chapter 1 | The Fall of the Brightest Star

A Look Back at the Origins of Dysfunctional Leadership

In my observations about leadership, I have come to believe that toxic and dysfunctional leaders share common tragic origins reaching back to the earliest stages of human existence. While modern leadership theory often ignores these ancient archetypes, they contain great wisdom. The biblical legend of Lucifer falling from heaven provides one of the most powerful metaphors for understanding the root causes of leadership dysfunction. By looking at this canonical story about dysfunction getting out of control, we can understand how unseen psychological problems can create chaos in organizations. Do we dare to see ourselves in this story?

In the Beginning: Noble Origins

The saga begins with Lucifer's noble origins. He was created as the most glorious and radiant archangel, unparalleled in beauty, knowledge, and talents among heavenly hosts. Bearing the name "Light Bearer," he served as a luminous beacon reflecting divine truth and wisdom.

As leader of the angelic choirs, Lucifer exercised tremendous influence in guiding worship and illuminating revelation. His countenance gleamed with uncontaminated light and creative fire. Lesser angels revered him as the brightest star, entrusting themselves to his vision. All honored him with his position at the Creator's right hand.

Yet this powerful position already carried the roots of dysfunctional behavior. The intoxication of power, privilege, genius, and reverence bred a grandiose self-perception. In the extreme privilege of his own light, darker recesses of insecurity and selfishness grew unchecked. Therein, the paradox took root - the brighter the star, the deeper its potential darkness.

The Poisoning of Pride

Pride poisons slowly before turning into severe dysfunction. As the favored angel, Lucifer took his talents and privileges for granted. He focused excessively on his own radiance rather than using it to serve others. His grand mission devolved into petty concerns of status and credit.

Resentment brewed as Lucifer fixated on his superiority over other angels. He grew to expect worship as his due rather than a gift freely given. A harmful sense of entitlement started corrupting his originally well-intentioned heart. It turned his wisdom into dysfunctional control over others.

This extreme dysfunction made him rebel against the truth. Even though he depended on divine gifts for his talents, he wrongly believed his greatness came from himself alone. As C.S. Lewis wrote, "It was through pride that the devil became the devil." His pride awakened the evil tendencies that had always existed inside him.

The Rebellion Against Truth

Dysfunction paved the road to Lucifer's rebellion against truth and catastrophic downfall. He came to see himself as greater than the divine himself. He believed the choir of angels rightfully owed him worship rather than the Creator. In his extreme arrogance, Lucifer refused to bow before any authority higher than himself. He rebelled against God's sovereignty, declaring himself the supreme ruler. Intoxicated by grandiose visions, he deceived a third of the angels to join his insurrection.

Blinded by profound narcissism, Lucifer could not perceive the disastrous consequences looming in his future. He couldn't see how unrealistic it was to try overthrowing an all-powerful authority. His talents turned from serving others into tools for control. Toxic behavior can only defend itself through more and more lies.

The Fall into Darkness

Arrogance unleashed madness. The fallen angel led forces against heaven itself. But his delusions of overthrowing omnipotence swiftly unraveled against the truth of reality. His reckless choices bore bitter fruit. Enlightenment evicted evil that day. God cast the dark angels out from eternal light into suffering and darkness. But Lucifer nursed his grudges rather than seeking redemption. His dysfunction festered further chaos and evil.

Twisting the truth, he pronounced his exile a victory. The darkness spreading from his broken spirit found no sanctuary. But still, he proselytized other souls into false promises. The rebellious angel kept descending further into darkness because those blinded by dysfunction could fall to any depths. Without intervention, those who fall drag multitudes down with them.

The Universal Cautionary Tale

Lucifer's fall provides a powerful cautionary tale. When inflamed with dysfunction, even the most brilliant can unleash terrible madness. Leadership qualities nurtured to serve others get repurposed for selfish gain. Privileges meant to serve others end up feeding selfishness.

Countless leaders through history have fallen prey to the same inner demons -- the grasping need for control, wealth, acclaim, and status. Like Lucifer, many gifted and well-intentioned leaders have the potential of being poisoned by greed, entitlement, and hunger for dominance. Levels meant to raise them up can become their demise.

We must guard our own hearts vigilantly against these parasites of the soul. If leaders ignore early mistakes, it can lead them to make excuses to act unethically. We must closely look at our dark inner tendencies before they take over completely. People can still change their path for the better if they catch themselves early enough before becoming a dysfunctional mess.

The Pathway Back to Grace

For all its darkness, Lucifer's legend also reveals pathways back to grace. Unlike Lucifer, with self-awareness and a change of heart, dysfunctional leaders can reclaim functionality. By helping others heal, we heal ourselves. Staying grounded in ethics and higher standards safeguards the soul from irrational passions.

Though the road remains long, positive change starts with the first step. Progress begins with the humility to concede when we've fallen, which then allows us to make things right again and begin an upward course. As Vaclav Havel wrote, "Hope is not the conviction that something will turn out well, but the certainty that something is worth doing no matter how it turns out." Lucifer forgot his gifts came from above, not within. But in remembering our shared brokenness, leaders can regain perspective beyond ego. By lifting each other, we can rise together.

The Leader's Journey

Dysfunction has shadowed leadership since humanity's earliest days. The line between dark and light cuts through every heart. But hope lives in higher standards than fear and ego. Functional leaders walk there. The path ahead promises hardship we cannot foresee. But know you don't walk alone. Others strive toward the same goal. Some failed before but kept going forward. We stumble. We rise. We walk on. I want to help leaders lead with wisdom, integrity, and compassion as guiding lights through darkness so that others can benefit from our functionality.

Chapter Summary:

- Lucifer's story symbolizes how even the most gifted leaders can unleash disaster when dysfunction goes unchecked. Intoxication with power and privilege bred darkness in his once brilliant light.

- Pride poisons slowly before cascading into severe dysfunction. Giving in to feelings of entitlement and pride early on turned Lucifer's functionality into selfish control over others. Resentment brewed as he lost perspective.

- Lucifer's hunger for power made him rebel against the truth. He became deluded into thinking he was above being responsible. He misled his followers into joining his rebellion. In this way, once the most talented angel fell from honor into disgrace.

- Lucifer's legend remains a universal cautionary tale. When inflamed by selfish passions, even the most talented lose their way and bring ruin. History shows many leaders perpetuated harm through similar inner demons of dysfunction.

- Lucifer also shows a redemptive path for those who rediscover higher callings beyond dysfunction. When leaders know themselves and are brave enough to do what's right, they can feel proud again. By lifting others up from darkness, we rise together. Our shared brokenness breeds compassion.

-------------------- **SECTION ONE** --------------------

Chapter 2 | The Bully Leader

Abrasive, Aggressive Leaders Who Rule by Intimidation and Create a Culture of Fear

In my decades of studying dysfunctional leaders, few personality types concern me more than the bully boss. This abrasive, aggressive leader rules through intimidation, manipulation and fear, infecting

Organizations and strangling creativity, performance and morale. Understanding the deep roots of their dysfunction becomes critical to steering bullies toward healthier paths before they irreparably damage culture. With self-awareness and courage, even the most dysfunctional leaders can find redemption through uplifting others, not defeating them. There is hope so long as interventions come before toxicity infiltrates across groups.

Early in my humble beginnings in pastoral ministry, my wife and I once worked on staff with a well-known pastor who had a world-wide television ministry. On the platform, he was a word merchant in his own right, but behind the scenes, he was known for the bullying of his staff over the smallest mistakes. He prided himself on keeping people "on their toes" through humiliating callouts. But the collateral damage was huge-- absenteeism and health issues rose as staff dreaded coming to work, anxiety skyrocketed as employees never could do anything right, and attrition shot through the roof, robbing the church of countless talents. Sadly, my wife and I eventually became a casualty of that war, and we learned to go where we were celebrated and not tolerated. To this day, his bully leadership style is still in full force. It was a sobering lesson on the stark difference between leadership through bullying versus inspiration.

In another case, a successful tech entrepreneur faced mass defections after her screaming tirades left people walking on eggshells daily. Though undoubtedly brilliant in her field, she profoundly lacked the basic emotional intelligence to positively engage her team. Any minor frustration unleashed a torrent of verbal abuse and profanity that battered morale. Talented employees fled rather than endure the soul-crushing cruelty. Only through intensive coaching on empathy and self-awareness did this leader finally reform her destructive habits. But not before immeasurable harm was done.

These cautionary examples underscore how even the most skilled individuals can spiral into toxic forces within organizations when they lead through raw intimidation and fear. Bully leaders create environments where people feel too threatened to think creatively or take chances. This crushes innovation. The brain's cognitive functions shut down in climates of constant anxiety and threat. Innovation dies, performance suffers, and unethical practices spread. Top talent inevitably votes with their feet.

In this chapter, we will examine the different manifestations of bully bosses--the controlling dictators, the tantrum tyrants, the hypercritical nitpickers, and the scheming manipulators. By understanding the deeply rooted psychology that fuels these dysfunctions, organizations can intervene with bully leaders and show them healthier paths before they irreparably damage culture and performance. However, such interventions must occur early or risk personnel and cultural destruction.

My Way or the Highway: The Controlling Bully

For years, I have heard too many stories of leaders who gravitate towards authoritarian control over their organizations. They firmly believe that merged power in their hands enables fast, decisive action. But this philosophy is dangerously short-sighted.

One instance dealt with a tech founder who had brilliant instincts for envisioning products but an equally absolutist view on managing his team. He rejected any suggestions or critiques as disloyal challenges to his authority. No decisions could occur without his explicit stamp of approval. On the surface, his firm operated efficiently in the short term. But troubling signs of dysfunction inevitably emerged.

Without diverse inputs and viewpoints, the founder's strategies gradually drifted out of touch with market realities. Employees just paid lip service to execute his orders that they had no stake in developing. Lack of oversight and accountability fueled fraud. The bully's unchecked self-conceit led him to dismiss clear research warnings, resulting in a catastrophic product failure that nearly bankrupted the company.

Another bully leader was a Fortune 500 CEO who ran a rigid command-and-control regime. His hyper-critical, my-way-or-the-highway leadership style crushed morale and motivation. The attrition of bright talent robbed the company of fresh thinking and innovation. After many years, disapproving employee surveys finally revealed just how depressingly dysfunctional the culture had become under his dominance.

Only then did the CEO begrudgingly accept the need to let go of the reins, delegate authority, and build up his team with positivity rather than fear.

These stories are all too familiar for those who have studied leadership pitfalls and organizational dysfunction. Dictatorial power breeds blind spots as critical feedback gets suppressed. Micromanaging drains initiative as teams lack autonomy and ownership. As the legendary Peter Drucker noted, good leaders don't make themselves indispensable--they multiply influence by intentionally developing others' strengths.

The Roman emperor Marcus Aurelius wisely wrote, "The key is to keep company only with people who uplift you." Every organization will have controlling personalities emerge. But with self-awareness, emotional intelligence, and wisdom, even rigid bully leaders can reform themselves to multiply influence through empowerment, not domination.

Yelling, Throwing Things, and Other Toddler Tactics

In my research into the dark side of leadership, I have encountered far too many driven, successful executives who fervently believed intimidation and outbursts of temper motivated their employees to superior performance. But time and again, their results told a far different story.

One hedge fund CEO proudly equated explosions of rage with strong, passionate leadership. When pressures peaked, he would frequently berate employees with profanity, insults, and unbridled fury, going so far as slamming fists on desks or even throwing things. In his mind, these intimidating eruptions effectively instilled the intensity and fear employees needed to excel under pressure. But his authoritarian strategy severely backfired over the long term:

- Turnover spiked as top talents understandably fled the toxic, abusive environment.
- Customer complaints skyrocketed as anxious, disengaged employees made errors and failed to provide adequate service.
- Team spirit and cooperation were destroyed. This left people acting only in their own self-interest rather than working together.

Only through intensive counseling did this CEO finally gain self-awareness of his deep rage-fueled insecurity and profound lack of emotional self-control. With great effort and support, he learned to replace traumatic outbursts with empathy, positivity, and motivational encouragement. As employees came to feel respected and valued, performance and morale indicators turned around.

The CEO came to realize after much inner work that respect freely given motivates people exponentially more than fear imposed through intimidation. His story proves positive change is possible from even deep-rooted behaviors, but requires ruthless self-honesty, tireless commitment, and often external help to permanently reform destructive habits.

The legendary leadership guru John C. Maxwell once coached a technology CEO notorious for public temper tantrums and berating employees at the slightest frustration. Under this reign of sustained abuse, product launches were continually damaged by mistakes and defective work as anxious people operated in fight or flight mode.

After stern feedback from dismayed investors on the CEO's destructive impacts, he finally acknowledged his deeply harmful behaviors. Through intensive mindfulness training and counseling, he slowly learned to pause, step back, and respond with wisdom and emotional intelligence rather than destructive reactive anger. This personal growth transformed the company culture.

As these sobering examples show, intimidation outbursts often stem from internal weakness and deep-seated fears, not authentic strength derived from one's values. But with courage, self-awareness, and commitment, even rage-prone leaders can tame their inner demons before it is too late and reach their full potential by earning influence through uplifting others rather than deflating them.

Nothing You Do Is Good Enough: The Hypercritical Bully

Some less severe bully leaders still rely too much on extreme criticism and unrealistic expectations even though it does not lead to excellence. They firmly believe that constant negative feedback, nitpicking, and impossible goals motivate high performance. But, research and experience reveal this punishing approach backfires.

I have frequently encountered leaders who default to endless criticism as their go-to management approach. They obsessively nitpick over insignificant details, constantly shift targets and move the goalposts, and freely hand out excessive negative feedback without any positive reinforcement to balance it.

These hypercritical bosses adamantly believe that relentless pressure stimulates higher performance. In their minds, employees absolutely need to be perpetually kept on their toes through ceaseless critique or they'll undoubtedly slack off. But decades of research conclusively demonstrate otherwise.

This very controlling approach and constantly pressuring the environment actually harms people's ability to perform well much more than it helps. When excellence is rewarded only with further nitpicking rather than recognition, employees quickly become discouraged. They gradually start disengaging entirely, doing the bare minimum required just to get by without examination. Customers soon suffer as workers feel neither empowered nor recognized for their efforts. Without accountability, unethical shortcuts get taken as people desperately try to meet unreasonable demands through bullying.

The best leaders know that lasting success requires both high standards as well as genuine care for people, including giving tough feedback but also praise for trying hard. They know that lifting people up through earned positive reinforcement consistently ignites great returns, whereas tearing them down through chronic denial breeds only resentment and paralysis. As Aristotle profoundly observed, educating the mind is meaningless without also educating the heart.

I once worked for a leader who only saw the bad in our team rather than the good that we were doing. It seemed that nothing we ever did was good enough for him. He micromanaged us and treated us like robots. Our team had no autonomy in thinking and it caused massive damage to our morale.

Over time, this hypercritical void of affirmation took an immense toll on our morale and performance. Our disengaged team quite rationally made only the minimum efforts required to complete tasks, accurately perceiving that any excellence would go unrewarded regardless. After one too many berating meetings by this bully leader, a co-worker and I mustered up the courage to get up and walk out on him, vowing never to be put through that again. This courageous move was a first for me and I have never allowed that situation to ever happen again in my work career.

Bully leaders can be taught to motivate through combining very high expectations with real empathy, including balancing blunt criticism with regularly noticing people's efforts. They can implement simple but powerful changes like beginning team meetings with quick shout-outs of appreciation and setting aside time for weekly recognition of people who moved key priorities forward. These small positives can substantially boost morale and performance.

We must remind bullying bosses that their penalizing methods are ultimately self-defeating, no matter their good intentions. In impatience, their desire for short-term results blinds them to the statistically proven backward impacts of their negative methods over time. Sustained progress depends not just on high standards but on emphasizing strengths-based constructive guidance, not magnifying weaknesses through blame and shame. Leaders able to inspire faith in people's potential and hidden talents, not doubts, best allow that potential to be fulfilled.

With self-awareness, emotional intelligence, and concerted effort, even the most hardened bully leaders can reform to multiply influence through abundant encouragement and wisdom, not habitual belittling. This is the key to achieving long-term success, fresh ideas, committed teams, and positive outcomes over time. But bullying habits must first be extinguished at the source.

Chapter Summary:

- Bully leaders use threats and aggression, which creates unsafe environments for people. Without intervention, their dysfunction spreads like cancer, destroying a healthy culture.
- Bully leaders merge their powers and stunt innovation, accountability, and development. Their dictatorship mindset damages morale and performance over time. But with self-awareness, even these leaders can learn to multiply influence through empowerment.
- Executives who rule through tantrums and rage instinctively equate fear with results. But trauma motivates neither loyalty nor excellence. By replacing outbursts with emotional intelligence and encouragement, leaders inspire sustainable gains.
- Hypercritical bosses adamantly believe that relentless negative feedback drives superior performance. But research shows such excessive criticism breeds only paralysis and resentment. Balance tough standards with authentic empathy and positive reinforcement to unleash potential.
- If dysfunctional bullying is addressed quickly, even severe cases can be improved, which makes leaders more effective. But lasting change requires ruthless self-examination, tireless inner work, and commitment to uplift people through inspiration, not intimidation.

Chapter 3 | The Clueless Leader

Close Look at Well-Meaning, Clueless Leaders Who make Decisions and are Inconsiderate of Others

Over the years, I've frequently encountered well-intentioned yet utterly clueless leaders. Similar to incompetent leaders mentioned later in this book, despite good motives, they breed disaster through poor decision-making stemming from blind spots, inadequate skills, and lack of touch with ground realities. While unintentional, the damage inflicted by these "rational fools" demands intervention before they steer organizations into icebergs. Through counsel, humility and securing missing capabilities, such leaders can gain the wisdom and judgment to convert intentions into positive outcomes. There is hope if they have the courage to see their shortcomings and commit to growth.

In this chapter, we'll explore the different facades of clueless leadership and their impacts on organizations. Understanding the roots of cluelessness positions us to guide these leaders toward the fulfillment of their potential. But without an awakening, even the brightest minds use power recklessly. There is a fine line between meaningless achievement and meaningful contribution.

Lacking Self-awareness: The Blind Leading the Blind

Self-awareness represents the key ingredient separating functional leaders from clueless ones. Defined simply, self-awareness means understanding one's strengths, weaknesses, blind spots and impacts on others. Leaders lacking this kind of insight into their limitations often unwittingly drive organizations downhill. Oblivious leaders misdiagnose critical challenges facing their teams. They overlook better solutions, staring them in the face. Most disastrously, they fail to recognize how their own behaviors and shortcomings actively degrade organizational culture and performance.

I have frequently encountered executives astonishingly disconnected from the reactions and impressions they sow in others day to day. Though boastful and quick to blame, these unaware leaders seem allergic to candid feedback illuminating their cluelessness. Without waking up, the most educated minds operate in blindness. Awakening requires humility - acknowledging we still have much to learn despite our accomplishments. Functional leaders stay open and eager to keep learning over time instead of becoming satisfied with the praise they get or having success in past achievements. Wise leaders understand they will never fully master everything in our complex world.

Asking for people's honest opinions shows leaders are self-assured instead of insecure. Mature leaders ask for constructive feedback to improve their perspectives, not just confirm what they already think. They know disagreements shared politely help them grow. However, clueless leaders automatically reject critical feedback that would make them evaluate themselves. By insulating selves inside protective bubbles, these clueless leaders stifle creativity and improvement. We experience the most personal growth when we confront that which we want to avoid.

Though far less satisfying than praise, constructive criticism provides essential feedback for personal improvement. Great leaders like Nelson Mandela and Bill Gates intentionally had people around them who questioned their ideas instead of just complimenting them. Hearing other people's views minimizes blind spots. By regularly asking for constructive opinions and seeing how their choices affect people, clueless leaders can gain more insight. They make two-way open communication normal. This sheds light on the gaps to be improved. Once you know your weaknesses, you can start addressing them. I have always lived by the mantra that we cannot change something if we do not know about it. Therefore, cultivating self-awareness separates empowering leaders from the clueless. Seeing your limitations frees up the ability to lead effectively. Even being clueless holds potential for improvement if acknowledged. Self-understanding removes barriers to growth.

Talking the Talk but Not Walking the Walk

Once, there was a newly appointed nonprofit CEO who envisioned bold outreach goals. She gave rousing speeches that energized supporters. However, she failed to implement the structures needed to deliver actual results. Despite soaring oratory skills, she struggled to secure funding, manage staff, or execute operationally on her grand vision. Employees and stakeholders quickly grew frustrated as her rhetoric far exceeded reality.

Big-picture vision matters little without disciplined execution. Leaders must not only paint an inspiring horizon but actively convert those lofty words into ground-level action. Doing so demands organizational strengths, managerial blocking, and tackling that do not automatically accompany charisma. Specifically, visionaries who can't execute operationally need training and coaching to develop skills like:

- Planning strategically and then delivering methodically
- Breaking bold visions into executable action plans
- Coordinating budgets, resources, and operational logistics
- Managing employee productivity and project timelines
- Monitoring progress and dynamically adjusting course
- Without these complementary abilities, such leaders breed disappointment and fragmented failure. However, pairing visionary big-picture thinkers with operationally minded leaders gifted at project execution forges tremendous balance. Together, they form complete skill sets needed to turn soaring dreams into realized impact. It is possible to go from having lots of big ideas but no structure to organized plans that achieve success.

Out of Touch Leaders

I once worked for an organization where a prominent leader, though very skilled, lacked self-awareness about how her actions impacted others. She would enter rooms expecting staff to immediately drop responsibilities and cater to her needs. Oblivious, she was clueless that people had other duties beyond serving her. Rather than empower her team, her behavior bred anxiety. Volunteers threatened to resign because of last-minute demands and scrapped plans. While well-intentioned, this leader's tunnel vision created a culture of frustration.

I eventually shared feedback with her about the low morale stemming from her out-of-touch style. But she struggled to receive constructive critique due to her cluelessness about how her ego-driven approach strained relationships and productivity. Despite her natural strengths, her self-focus undermined the organization's progress. Even though I tried my best, her refusal to listen and improve herself showed that she would not make the necessary changes to improve the culture. With sadness, the only choice I had was to move on to a new opportunity and I realized positive change would only arise from a new generation of leadership.

Even highly competent, seasoned leaders, over time lose touch with ground-level realities. Leaders become isolated in executive suites, listening only to minions who tell them manipulated information to make them happy. Vital feedback from the frontlines gets muddled as it passes through layers of bureaucracy. Also, as big organizations keep growing, top leaders are even more likely to lose touch as they get further removed from understanding their employees' real day-to-day problems.

However, competent, self-aware leaders who want to stay connected can intentionally keep learning about frontline realities, even after they get high positions. Great leaders make sure they regularly spend time with lower-level employees and customers to get honest opinions that test their beliefs and give fresh understanding. They do this by talking to frontlines directly, having other managers share staff feedback, anonymously surveying workers, and listening to customer calls. By walking distribution centers and store floors, they grasp market dynamics and competitive threats missed within their corner offices. Leaders who listen to ground-level workers, as well as higher-ups, can gain critical knowledge that prevents them from losing touch. There are ways to stay strongly connected to real situations so decisions make sense.

Smart Leaders Who Outsmart Themselves

When a gifted CEO had sailed through advanced degree programs and joined Mensa, he prided himself on making elaborate and impressively sophisticated strategies. But when implemented in the real world, unpredictable factors and unintended consequences consistently derailed these clever plans. Although he was extremely smart, his overly clever plans consistently didn't work when put into complex, unpredictable, real-world conditions.

Even though a very high IQ gives some benefits for strategy, it doesn't prevent leaders from coming up with plans much more complicated than are usable. Often, the most brilliant leaders outsmart themselves through highly ornate complexity bordering on dysfunction. They apply game theories and cunningly conceived tactics with little concept of how real human psychology, irrational emotions, and uncontrollable external forces will undermine the clever plan constructed in their heads.

When things are chaotic, having a deep understanding of what is going on is more helpful than just being very smart analytically. Rather than complex strategies, wise leaders develop simple but sturdy frameworks to navigate uncertainty. By getting input from a wide range of people, leaders gain more complete views on situations. Combining different ways of thinking gives decisions greater depth and insight. The savviest leaders neither hoard authority nor rely solely on solitary brainpower. They distribute leadership across empowered teams with collective wisdom greater than any individual. A reliable course correction is needed when complexity becomes the problem rather than the cure.

With self-awareness, emotional intelligence, and humility, even remarkably clueless leaders can gain the wisdom, judgment, and listening skills needed to convert good intent into positive real-world impact. However, this depends on leaders being brave enough to acknowledge gaps in their abilities and dedicate themselves fully to improving rather than protecting their reputations. Those surrounding clueless leaders also play a pivotal role by providing candid counsel and filling knowledge or experience gaps.

I remain hopeful about the clueless leader being surrendered with quality people and transformed. However, late in life, perspective is gained, and the upward journey never truly ends. Each day brings new opportunities to learn if we walk in humility. The upside of leadership is a lifelong journey rather than a fixed destination. If clueless leaders realize that smarts without care for people and morals harm more than helps, even the most oblivious can still achieve excellence and lead impactfully. But without this honesty, even geniuses misuse authority in ways that get things done but lack purpose.

Chapter Summary:

- It's very common for people to get promoted to jobs that are beyond what they can handle. Leaders often get tapped for jobs they lack the skills to fulfill. Without intervention, good intentions produce negative results. But with humility and development, potential can be achieved.

- Visions without practical plans are meaningless. Leaders who give great motivational speeches need basic organizational skills to turn those words into actual success. Combining those who envision big ideas with those who know how to build step-by-step details creates powerful partnerships.

- Leaders lose touch with frontline challenges over time. Having direct dialogue with lower-level staff, listening to their honest feedback, and anonymously surveying them gives leaders unbiased opinions about real challenges faced. Leaders in power can always find ways to reconnect with on-the-ground realities if they stay humble.

- Sheer intellect offers little immunity from over-engineering solutions. The most brilliant leaders sometimes outsmart themselves through excessive complexity disconnected from real-world dynamics. When things are chaotic, having a straightforward but adaptable strategy based on inputs from different people allows more effective leadership when situations are uncertain.

- With self-awareness, emotional intelligence and humility, even remarkably clueless leaders can gain the wisdom, judgment and listening skills to convert good intentions into positive real-world impacts. It is never too late to commit to personal growth, no matter how high one has risen.

Chapter 4 | The Incompetent Leader

Leaders who are Bad at Their Jobs and Fail to Effectively Manage People or Operations

With very similar characteristics as the clueless leaders, incompetence manifests in many ways - the unskilled, the disengaged, the untrained. But the result remains the same: dysfunction and disillusionment. In this chapter, let us examine the different faces of incompetent leadership and their impacts. While these leaders likely have good intentions, their weaknesses and gaps create dysfunction. Only self-awareness, humility and commitment to growth can correct their course.

The Peter Principle in Action: Promoting Incompetence

A business consultant told the story of a fun-loving bank manager who was promoted to president based more on likability than actual leadership capabilities. Predictably, he floundered in this elevated role, making disjointed directives that confused his team. Morale and performance declined sharply as he moved from crisis to crisis. It was a textbook case of the Peter Principle in action.

This concept, developed by educator Laurence Peter, observes that personnel tend to rise to their "level of incompetence" in hierarchical organizations. Essentially, they get promoted based on strengths in their current role that don't automatically translate into competencies needed for the next level up. We falsely presume capabilities transfer, only to be proven wrong. As a student of leadership for decades, I have seen this play out across organizations of all sizes and industries.

A capable sales representative promoted to senior management solely because of strong individual contributor metrics, floundering without empathy or emotional intelligence required to lead a team. An engineer promoted to operations director, struggling to transition from a tactical doer to a strategic planner. The mismatch of skills to responsibilities breeds tension and dysfunction.

We wrongly assume excellence in one role guarantees effectiveness in the next. However, leading people demand different talents beyond just professional expertise in a field. Without properly assessing leadership capabilities, talented individuals end up in roles where they repeat past mistakes. Intelligence and credentials do not automatically transfer to strategic wisdom or interpersonal skills.

As Peter Drucker wisely cautioned, we must vigilantly match people to positions that align with their strengths rather than forcing square pegs into round holes. This takes humility and subtlety from those in authority, not simplistic formulas based on tenure or past metrics. Empowering competent, engaged leadership requires objectivity about capabilities.

Rushing promotions without proper equipping for next-level challenges damages morale and performance. But done with care, challenging people just beyond their comfort zone grows abilities. Mentorship and leadership training cultivate skills for new demands. When incompetence stems from inexperience, not negligence, investment in development bears fruit.

Without intentional development to fill critical skill gaps, today's star performer often becomes tomorrow's overwhelmed leader. But these blind spots do not need to be fatal. Assessing potential gaps, seeking sage counsel, and proactively investing in developing leadership development can minimize deficiencies even later in the game. Incompetence is not necessarily a permanent sentence. With humility and perseverance, even those unequipped for responsibilities thrown upon them can grow into competence - and beyond. This gives optimism for change if incompetent leaders are brave enough to see their flaws and work on improving.

Asleep at the Wheel: The Disengaged Leader

In my career, I have encountered and heard stories of many intelligent, seasoned leaders who nonetheless demonstrate shocking disengagement, neglecting even basic responsibilities. Despite sound expertise, they remain asleep at the wheel.

One executive took months to approve projects while avoiding major strategic decisions altogether. Stumbling through meetings distracted and unprepared, this leader's rudderless approach left the team directionless and dismayed. Though surveys exposed this negligence, the executive deflected responsibility with empty promises to improve. It was only after an ultimatum from the board that he finally committed to fully assuming the responsibilities of his role.

Such detachment stems not from a lack of skills but a lack of passion. As Peter Drucker observed, "No institution can survive if it needs geniuses or supermen to manage it." Great leadership is not brilliance alone but engaging deeply with purpose. Reigniting passion cures disengagement. Sometimes, routine dulls the sense of mission. Renewed purpose realigns leaders to wholeness. By inspiring others through service, great leaders stay meaningfully engaged at the wheel. This profoundly impacts organizations in a positive way.

Leaders can rediscover passion through self-care practices that rejuvenate mental health and emotional reserves. Spending time mentoring and bonding with team members also recharges meaning. When a lack of passion stems from lacking meaning, leaders can reignite motivation.

With support and perseverance, leaders can overcome apathy to fully inhabit roles again. The path back from disengagement requires intention, self-awareness, and committing to a renewed direction. But by first strengthening their sense of purpose, discouraged leaders regain can energy to excel.

Training? We Don't Need Stinking Training!

I have often seen a common mistake in organizations-- leaders are given responsibility without proper leadership training. Just having professional experience or intellect alone does not provide someone with the distinct interpersonal and strategic skills essential for great management. This gap breeds dysfunction.

One leader, despite a successful track record, alienated her new team through emotional outbursts, impatience, and public criticism once promoted. Lacking any management training, her self-awareness could not catch up to new responsibilities overnight. Only intensive coaching helped develop empathy, communication, and motivational skills on the job. Proper leadership development beforehand may have averted much damage.

We must intentionally foster excellence through training, mentoring, and coaching at every career stage. As John Quincy Adams observed, "If your actions inspire others to dream more, learn more, do more, and become more, you are a leader." But these abilities do not arise by accident. They require investment.

There was an organization that assumed directors naturally would handle increased responsibilities upon promotion to VP. By not properly equipping them with new skills beforehand, many flailed, sowing confusion. Only after correcting this gap did their capabilities catch up with their titles. Just like muscles, leadership skills must be exercised to grow stronger. Proper training builds the right habits early on. As Simon Sinek wrote, "Leadership is not about being in charge. It's about taking care of those in your charge." Let us honor that duty by developing leaders at every step of the journey.

Surrounded by Yes-men: How Incompetence Persists

In working with organizations plagued by incompetent leadership, I've observed a troubling dynamic--deficient leaders surrounding themselves with enablers or yes-men rather than truth-tellers. Craving ego validation over accountability, these leaders stack the inner circle with minions focused on praise rather than honesty or accuracy. By blocking out criticism, their limitations go unaddressed and their false competence compounds, spreading dysfunction.

Such willful blindness to feedback brings immense risk, as Margaret Heffernan cautioned: "Willful blindness doesn't happen overnight or to just anyone. It is a process--one that requires, if not a conscious decision, then at least some level of choice."

Functional leaders seek truth-telling and self-betterment above ego protection. With courageous humility, they confront brutal facts about deficiencies and then commit to growth. As Socrates said, "The unexamined life is not worth living." Functional leaders embody this. While incompetent leaders breed frustration through denial, by embracing honest feedback with resilience, they can transform weaknesses into strengths. But this first takes facing harsh truths, then tenaciously striving to overcome them through learning and development.

Surrounding leaders with wisdom and truth kindles their growth. Therein lies the path for the dormant potential to be realized. With humility and perseverance, even struggling leaders can emerge renewed. But it first takes examining where we are resisted or blind, then making choices toward wholeness.

Leadership Emerges from Within

Becoming an impactful leader begins with self-examination, introspection, and a commitment to continual growth. Deficient leaders often lack self-awareness of how their behaviors sow dysfunction. Transforming this requires courageously confronting our limitations with radical honesty and then doing the difficult inner work and skill-building needed to overcome them. As Peter Drucker counseled, "Leaders grow; they are not made." Growth emerges from within through ongoing self-development and a willingness to be shaped by difficult experiences. Knowledge and expertise alone do not automatically translate into great leadership. Those capabilities must be exercised and refined to address the complex demands of guiding organizations and people. We lead by who we become, not merely what we know.

Outgrowing incompetence requires going to the root. A title does not automatically make one a leader; authority is granted only through the consent of those being led. Hence, leaders must examine the inconsistencies between external structures and internal readiness, then humbly commit to closing gaps through mentorship, training, introspection, and lived experience. There are no shortcuts to becoming a better leader.

Rather than propping up false images, functional leaders candidly assess deficiencies and blind spots, then take responsibility for making changes. Protecting the ego makes us stagnant; honest learning expands our potential to address new challenges. Great leaders are continuous students, not static gurus. Growth propels their leadership.

The Donkey in The Well

An old fable tells of a donkey that falls into a well, braying miserably for hours as the farmer tries to figure out how to get him out. Finally, the farmer decides the donkey is old and the well provides a reasonable grave. He starts shoveling dirt into the well.

At first, the donkey feels the falling dirt hit his back and panics even more. But at some point, he makes a defining choice - with each shovel of dirt, he shakes it off and steps up. The once dire circumstance becomes empowering as he rises higher with each layer of dirt, eventually able to climb right out of the well.

Leaders facing the dirt of criticism or exposure of deficiencies similarly have a choice-either succumb beneath the scorn and demands, or empower themselves to shake them off and step up. If we let the dirt weigh upon us or overwhelm our identity, we remain stuck. But by viewing it as pathways for growth, deficiencies become opportunities to build higher competencies that lift our leadership ever upward. Outer circumstances do not define leaders. Our response to life's dirt does.

With this resilience and commitment to growth, incompetent leaders can emerge renewed, converting past mistakes into wisdom. The heaviest dirt, once shaken off, becomes the strongest foundation to stand upon. But this first takes courageously admitting where we have fallen short, then humbly doing the work of restoration--of trust, skills, vision, and hope.

Leading Through Crisis

When organizations face sudden crises or challenges, deficient leaders often crumble where exceptional ones emerge. Their character and capabilities are tested under fire. This trial reveals who can guide teams through difficult moments versus who compounds anxiety and dysfunction in the heat of pressure. Those lacking emotional and strategic maturity falter.

In such times of uncertainty, leaders tempted to control and overreact often underperform those able to stay calm, exude confidence and focus teams with a clear vision. Capabilities forged through experience and self-awareness make the difference. Confident leaders steady the nerves when incompetent ones unravel. They bring out the best in people rather than fear.

And in times where quick strategic pivots become necessary, competent leaders can more smoothly adapt, while inept ones flounder. Crises expose gaps where further development is needed. Wise leaders recognize these blind spots and commit to growth rather than denial.

But just as muscles strengthen under resistance training, crises present opportunities to grow leadership skills like strategic agility, stakeholder communication, and principled decision-making. Those who leverage difficulty for self-betterment emerge stronger. Leaders are not defined by the crisis but by how they respond to it. Great leaders convert trials into breakthroughs. True leadership emerges the strongest during difficult times.

Restoring Trust

When incompetent leadership causes team dysfunction, restoring organizational health requires rebuilding broken trust. Trust forms the foundation of a cohesive culture, and when leaders demonstrate negligence or poor character, they must humbly regain team confidence through accountability, transparency, and demonstrated commitment to improvement.

Rather than issue blanket apologies and empty promises, leaders must honestly examine the root cultural and capability issues that contributed to deficiencies, then put in place systems for accountability and communication to track improvement. They must solicit feedback, take ownership of growth, and follow through on development plans. The only consistency in rebuilding trust earns back team respect.

In my experience working in organizations with competence issues, I've seen leadership rehabilitation succeed through a few key practices:

- publicly owning the problems and committing to transparency
- investing in resources geared toward training and mentoring
- increasing team empowerment and autonomy
- decentralizing control wherever possible
- often communicating around progress and milestones

Above all, leaders must embody the change they wish to see, leading by example with care and character. This builds the right spirit to fuel a cultural turnaround. A fish rots from the head down. Likewise, restoration begins from the top.

The Outer Reflects the Inner

Functional leadership understands organizational culture flows outward from the inner life of leaders. Deficiencies that manifest in poor business outcomes first take root internally--in the attitudes, assumptions, and emotional health of those steering the ship. Rehabilitating incompetent leadership requires addressing these heart issues.

As Peter Drucker wisely noted, "Culture eats strategy for breakfast." The most brilliant plans fail when leaders lack emotional health or spiritual grounding. In my desire to see transformation in organizational culture, getting underneath poor strategies, processes and behaviors to realign mindsets, motivations and shared values is key. Just fixing surface issues without understanding root causes leads to superficial fixes. The inner game drives the outer results.

This begins with self-awareness. Self-examination to unearth fears, insecurities, limiting beliefs and false narratives, which influence poor decisions, allows inner obstacles to be overcome.

As psychoanalyst Carl Jung said, "Until you make the unconscious conscious, it will direct your life and you will call it fate." The inner world shapes leadership.

Beyond self-knowledge, building emotional reserves through self-care and spirituality helps leaders avoid depletion and remain grounded. These inner resources sustain the resilience required to overcome incompetence in the face of challenges.

Chapter Summary:

- People often get promoted to their level of incompetence when skills that yield success don't transfer to promoted roles. Assessing capability gaps honestly, rather than assuming that excellence transfers is key to appropriate placement and development.

- Disengaged leaders confuse people because they allow their abilities to go unused. Reigniting passion realigns them. Renewed purpose through self-care, team connections, and focusing on uplifting others reengages stalled leaders. With support, they can inhabit roles fully again.

- Incompetent limitations are best addressed early through training and mentorship. Assuming leaders will simply grow into roles without thoughtful development fails individuals and culture. Equipping must evolve with responsibilities. Growth depends on continually expanding capabilities.

- Incompetent leaders rationalize poor performance rather than seeking feedback for growth. They surround themselves with enablers who coddle their egos rather than truth-tellers caring enough to candidly address their dysfunction. This willful blindness solidifies limitations. But by embracing criticism with tenacity, leaders can overcome it through learning.

- Restoring organizational trust following incompetence requires accountability, development, and reforming underlying systems. But culture flows from leadership's inner life. So sustainable change reaches beneath surface behaviors to realign motivations, self-awareness, and emotional health.

Chapter 5 | The Micromanager Leader

The Examination of the Toxic Impact of the All-Seeing Eye

Nothing disheartens teams faster than micromanagement--the excessive obsession with controlling minor details. Micromanagers hover constantly, dictating processes and strangling flexibility and creativity. Though well-intended, their fixation on rigid methods demoralizes employees and limits possibilities.

In this chapter, we will examine the behaviors and motivations of micromanager leaders. Though they pursue productivity, their extreme supervision achieves the opposite by smothering creativity, autonomy and development. By recognizing over-controlling tendencies in ourselves, we can shift to empowering management that unlocks potential.

Micromanagers operate from deep distrust, criticizing endlessly to avoid delegating. But functional leaders do the opposite--they coach people up, not control them down. Wisdom understands that loosening the reins takes us further than tightening them. Rather than enforce conformity, effective leaders nurture growth.

My experience shows that micromanagers drain possibilities from people and organizations. However, self-awareness allows leaders to transition from controlling everything to empowering everyone. Progress depends on elevating the capabilities of the team. The fullest harvests come not by fixating on each seed but by enabling each one to flourish freely. When these changes are made, leaders migrate from micro to macro.

Excessive Control Over Details

The micromanager is consumed with controlling even the most minor details. Rather than focus on high-level goals and vision, they impose their authority over routine operational decisions better left to their team. This excessive fixation on dogmatic methods severely restricts their team's autonomy. By dictating the "how" behind all tasks, these dysfunctional leaders leave no room for individual judgment or initiative.

Micromanagers rationalize that their intense supervision enhances productivity and perfection. But in reality, preoccupation with bureaucratic processes hinders both speed and quality. By disempowering workers, extreme oversight frustrates them more than it motivates them.

These leaders demand a say in every minor decision, refusing to delegate tasks within employees' capabilities. But great leaders do the opposite - they release them to be free to do what they were hired to do. Excessive supervision backfires by constraining skill growth needed to eventually work independently at higher levels.

Finally, micromanagers enforce strict protocols as the illusion of control. But excessive adherence to rigid procedures sacrifices responsiveness and common sense. In turbulent times, fixation on inflexible steps rather than outcomes proves to be a liability.

Mastery requires less command and more guiding vision. Functional leaders provide just enough structure to align efforts without imposing total control that restricts creativity. Wisdom understands that loosening the reins propels people much further than tightening them ever could.

Lack of Trust in Their Team

At its core, micromanagement stems from a fundamental lack of trust in the team and motivation. Micromanagers chronically second-guess their team members due to assuming incompetence or ill intent. Rather than grant autonomy, these leaders closely monitor workers out of suspicion. They frequently question decisions and undermine confidence in subordinates' judgement. Criticism flows freely, while praise remains scarce.

Micromanagers also intensely scrutinize why tasks are done in certain ways. They interpret creativity as defiance and simple errors as deep flaws. Workers get demoralized trying to satisfy expectations of perfection. This lack of trust severely limits employee empowerment.

Micromanagers refuse to meaningfully delegate critical tasks and authority. They prefer centralizing decisions to avoid perceived risks of autonomy. But this disempowers workers from developing leadership skills. Functional leaders do the opposite--they demonstrate deep trust in people through granting latitude and responsibility. They coach individuals toward the capacity to handle greater independence down the road. Wisdom understands that letting go propels people forward. But micromanagers cannot bring themselves to loosen the reins despite the benefits. They allow their own fear and suspicion to override investing in human potential. Until core trust issues get addressed, their fixation on control will persist as a barrier to excellence.

Stifling Creativity and Growth

By severely limiting autonomy, micromanagement stifles creativity, problem-solving and individual growth within teams. The obsessive focus on standardized processes and oversight prevents the flexibility required for innovation to blossom. Workers under dysfunctional micromanagers lack the freedom to experiment with solutions. They come to rely on upper-level approval for basic decisions rather than using their own judgment. This breeds frustration and learned helplessness rather than creativity.

Left unchecked, micromanagers create unnecessary bureaucracies centered around themselves. Processes multiply to reinforce their control and validate their self-importance. Employees get bogged down executing redundant protocols. Excessive oversight also hinders professional development. People improve through exercising independent judgment, even imperfectly. But micromanagers deprive team members of such growth opportunities. This stunts individual potential and capacity to handle greater responsibility.

Unsurprisingly, talent retention suffers under micromanagement. Talented, creative people will not tolerate highly controlling environments that deprive them of freedom and autonomy. Rather than contributing their gifts, they take them elsewhere. Only conformists willing to abandon autonomy remain. Functional leaders do the opposite--they focus on unleashing capability by fostering independence balanced with accountability. They understand that empowering environments allow people to blossom, enhancing innovation and cultivating future leadership.

Communication Bottlenecks

Micromanagers frequently hoard information to solidify power rather than empower others. By controlling data flows, they reinforce reliance upon themselves for all decisions. But this creates significant communication bottlenecks. Vital information gets bottlenecked at the top. Micromanagers insist on personally vetting even basic communications. But they can't handle too much, so their ability to respond gets overwhelmed.

This over-centralization breeds organizational chaos. Team members waste critical time seeking input on routine matters. Simple decisions face long delays waiting on the leader's approval. Progress stalls at the chokepoint of their whims.

Micromanagers also construct elaborate hierarchies requiring excessive signoffs. Even internal coordination faces layers of redundant oversight. Staff expend more energy navigating bureaucracy than driving outcomes. Functional leaders avoid such dysfunction by distributing authority across empowered, accountable teams. They share information transparently to inform decision-making at all levels. Rather than constrain flows, they open channels and get out of the way. True leadership must balance oversight with efficiency. Micromanagers fail to grasp that their fixation on control severely obstructs operational rhythms. But unlocking progress depends on aligning authority with capability--not bottling it at the top.

Damaging Morale and Relationships

By undermining autonomy, micromanagers inflict great damage on team morale, emotional wellbeing and interpersonal relationships. Their corrosive impact accumulates until reaching toxic levels. They also erode confidence and self-worth through excessive criticism and second-guessing. Team members feel monitored under perpetual surveillance. Even small errors draw rebukes from the dysfunctional micromanager. This anxiety stifles thinking and initiative.

People come to resent constant oversight and the implication that they require intense supervision. Creativity gets constrained by managers prescribing rigid "hows" behind all tasks. Team cohesion frays under bureaucratic layers, breeding friction and turf wars. Micromanagers rationalize these costs as necessary tradeoffs. But their extreme focus on control blinds them to the destructive human impacts. Morale spirals downward, turnover costs climb, and resentment festers.

However, functional leaders set overall goals while giving their team responsibility for choosing how they are achieved. They provide high-level guidance and resources and then trust people to excel. Wisdom understands that less organizational touch from micromanagers propels the highest performance over time. Despite short-term risks, letting go liberates human potential.

Transitioning From Micro to Macro

Transforming micromanager leaders requires brutal self-awareness and feedback from others. Leaders must recognize their own controlling tendencies before mindsets shift. Self-examination should evaluate the real motives behind strict methods—possibly insecurity? Perfectionism? Fear of allowing mistakes? The causes of over-control must be confronted.

Top leaders must then coach these micromanagers on transitioning from command-and-control to coaching and empowering. Training should build trust in people, comfort with ambiguity, and skills in delegating and developing others. Organizations must also review incentive structures that inadvertently encourage micromanaging. Basing job stabilityand pay solely on strict rules encourages controlling behavior.But judging leaders on real-world outcomes demands giving more authority to teams.

Finally, mindset changes come through repeatedly experiencing the upside of empowering people with freedom. As leaders loosen their grips and focus on outcomes rather than methods, the benefits become self-evident. Wisdom dawns gradually. In totality, the journey requires exchanging the illusion of total control for the reality of trust in others. By leaving fate in sight but releasing the reins, leaders unlock exponential potential in people.

These dysfunctional micromanager leaders impede the very productivity it seeks by disempowering people. But, self-awareness allows leaders to move from controlling everything to empowering everyone. This liberation mentality focuses on outcomes rather than procedures. It trades command for coaching and develops future leaders. By loosening grips, leaders amplify creativity and ownership. This action replaces suspicion with trust.

The fullest harvests come not by fixating on each seed but by enabling each one to flourish freely. Therein, leaders relinquish the immediate for the ultimate, the fear of failure for the courage of growth. For once they experience the soaring possibilities unleashed through empowerment, leaders shed microscopes for telescopes. Their horizons expand from the immediate to the infinite. Progress unfolds through liberating human potential, not controlling it.

Chapter Summary:

- Micromanagers obsess over controlling minor details, strangling autonomy and innovation. By dictating processes, they demoralize teams and limit possibilities. But their extreme oversight tries achieving productivity through counterproductive means.

- Micromanagement stems from deep distrust in people's abilities and motives. This chronic suspicion breeds excessive oversight along with bottlenecks hoarding authority. But functional leaders demonstrate trust by empowering teams balanced with accountability.

- By severely limiting independence, micromanagers constrain creativity, problem-solving, individual growth, and responsibility. Their obsessive control breeds bureaucracy and conformity rather than innovation and development.

- Centralizing authority causes massive communication dysfunction. Information gets bottlenecked and simple decisions face endless delays seeking approval. But progress depends on transparency, delegated capability and streamlined flows.

- The cumulative damage on morale, relationships and emotional health reaches toxic levels. But with self-awareness and yielding control, leaders can instead focus on vision and outcomes by empowering human potential.

Therein exponential gains become possible after the long road from micro to macro.

Chapter 6 | The Narcissistic Leader

Examination of Egotistical, Self-Absorbing Leaders Who Put Their Own Interests First

In my leadership research, few dysfunctional traits concern me more than narcissism--an excessive self-focus that erodes judgment and morale. Narcissistic leaders feel entitled to special treatment, prestige, and validation. Their oversized egos and insatiable craving for affirmation sow chaos within teams. They leave damaged organizations and bruised spirits in their wake.

In this chapter, we will examine the deep drivers of narcissism, its rippling impacts on culture, and whether redemption is possible for such leaders. By illuminating the destructive rooted psychology behind narcissism, we can intervene earlier before permanent wreckage is done.

The Empty Core Behind Narcissism's False Self

Narcissism stems from suppressed shame and insecurity. Narcissists construct false outward selves to chase the validation and status they desperately seek but which always eludes them. This futile quest causes them to insulate their egos from criticism that betrays their self-image. They demand loyalty and praise from subordinates to support their fragile inner esteem. But this need for constant external validation only amplifies their inner doubts.

Narcissists exploit others as instruments for their ego goals. But their relationships remain shallow, empty of empathy. They leave behind broken people and fractured organizations--mere collateral damage in their thirst for glory.

The Narcissist's Toxic Impact on Culture

Narcissistic leaders cast long, dark shadows over organizational culture. Their volatile egos breed insecurity and fear among those who follow them. Critics face retaliation. When narcissistic leaders tolerate incompetent followers, it often leads to a culture where the unethical and untalented get promoted. This warps incentives and accountability within the organization.

Narcissists take credit for others' successes but deflect blame for their failures. Their lack of empathy spawns a callous and politicized environment. Consumed with advancing their own status, they fracture teams in their wake. Over time, narcissists detach themselves from reality, causing recklessness and corruption and often culminating in scandal, downfall, and organizational ruin. But they rationalize away responsibility and feel no remorse, failing to take into consideration the human toll of their actions.

It's All About Me: Understanding Narcissistic Personality Disorder

Early on in my full-time pastoral ministry, I worked for a pastor with extreme narcissistic tendencies. He demanded the staff to treat him like a king, relishing lavish privileges on him, claimed sole credit for successes, and raged when challenged. The entire organization suffered greatly because of his ego-driven antics, and no one had the courage to stand up against him for fear of losing their job. He had zero empathy for letting people go under the guise that he was superior and everyone else was peasants that he controlled. As of the writing of this book, he is still in pastoral control of this church and, according to contacts that are still there on staff, his narcissistic behavior is worse than it ever has been. Over two decades have passed since my wife and I worked for this leader, and the church is about half its size with no sign of the pastor ever changing his ways or becoming a functional leader.

Narcissism exists on a spectrum. Mild self-absorption differs from the clinical pathology of narcissistic personality disorder (NPD), characterized by:

- Grandiose sense of self-importance and entitlement
- Obsession with power, brilliance, and physical appearances
- Lack of empathy and willingness to exploit people for personal gain
- Requirement for excessive admiration and validation
- Hypersensitivity to criticism, with extravagant displays of rage

My studies have shown that narcissistic tendencies often stem from childhood experiences and ingrained personality traits. Specifically, emotional neglect in the early years leaves children seeking validation through external sources like fame and status. Children praised by parents only for their natural abilities rather than hard work, can develop fragile self-esteem that depends heavily on external validation from others.

Furthermore, narcissists often harbor profound insecurities and fears of inadequacy underneath their grandiose displays, using boastfulness to cover up deep-seated feelings of inferiority.

Finally, some narcissists tragically display ingrained antisocial behaviors like deceit, aggression, and willingness to exploit others, reflecting stunted conscience development. By understanding these rooted drivers, we gain insights into constructively influencing narcissistic leaders away from their most damaging instincts.

The Toll of Narcissistic Leadership

Research has shown that there is an immense toll that narcissistic leaders have on organizations if left unchecked over time. Specifically, their need for control breeds toxic cultures marked by fear, silenced criticism, and poor communication. Rejecting critical feedback while surrounding themselves with yes-men leads narcissists toward strategic blunders. Team members feel exhausted and demoralized, catering to a narcissist's whims, and these feelings harm talent retention. Unethical behavior spreads as narcissists believe rules don't apply to them, rationalizing their misconduct.

Eventually, employees publicly expose this leader's disruptive behaviors, tarnishing reputations and deterring essential investors, partners, and recruits. The one upside is that narcissists' skill at charming stakeholders helps them ascend into leadership roles initially. But this glosses over fatal flaws that eventually wreak havoc once in power. Understanding these dangerous organizational impacts underscores the necessary steps of restraining narcissistic leaders as early on as possible in their tenure.

Can Narcissistic Leaders Change?

It depends on whether a narcissist can really change. Mild narcissistic traits may improve with counseling and mentoring on emotional intelligence. But full narcissistic pathology reflects ingrained personality, intensified by power, and proves largely resistant to change. Here are some tips for mitigating narcissistic leaders' damage:

- Seek early diagnosis. Use clinical criteria to assess if narcissism exceeds manageable levels.
- Establish oversight. Narcissists thrive on unilateral power. Checks and balances restrict abuses.
- Set clear conduct policies. Hold these leaders accountable for violations, regardless of rank.
- Insist on transparency. Open records, financial reporting and processes prevent the concealment of misdeeds.
- Provide alternative feedback channels. Workers need to feel psychologically safe to share feedback and opinions honestly with upper level leaders.
- Reward ethics and teamwork. Incentives should reinforce organizational values, not self-interest.
- Maintain vigilant governance. Narcissists exploit blind trust. Proactive oversight is vital.

Taking All the Credit: Narcissists' Need for Recognition

There was an arrogant tech founder who took full credit for his engineering team's innovations. Their breakthroughs fueled his fame and fortune. But privately, he ridiculed them as expendable drones. This insatiable hunger for recognition reveals a core narcissistic trait--assuming credit while denying it to others. Despite little direct involvement, narcissists crave the spotlight for collective achievements. But this "glory hog" behavior has consequences:

- Talent exodus: Star players resent leaders taking credit for their contributions and leave.

- Morale deterioration: Employees feel disrespected, used, and unappreciated by glory-hog leaders. Resentment destroys engagement.

- Stifled collaboration: People hoard information that might enhance the leader's image rather than cooperatively sharing knowledge.

- Poisoned culture: Narcissist leaders signal that loyalty to them overrides fairness or truth. This fosters cut-throat competition.

- Reputation decline: A leader seen as self-promoting at the expense of others earns distrust and ridicule. Their personal brand suffers.

As the great servant leader Robert Greenleaf wrote, "True leadership emerges from those whose primary motivation is a deep desire to help others." But narcissists are motivated only by helping themselves. Restraining their credit-hogging requires systemic solutions--publicly acknowledging team contributions, emphasizing that success depends on collaboration, defining and rewarding ethical and team-oriented behaviors, discretely seeking feedback on the leader's trust and integrity, and ensuring rewards flow to those doing the work.

With support, mildly narcissistic leaders may temper their grandiose instincts and instead channel them towards inspiring group achievements. However, those with engrained narcissistic pathology will only co-opt interventions for personal gain. In such severe cases, eliminating them altogether may become the only viable solution to protect the organization from future harm.

Rules Don't Apply to Me: Narcissistic Arrogance

In another example, a CEO believed rules only applied to regular people, not important people like himself. He fired compliance officers who questioned his practices. His entitled mindset rationalized bribing officials, misusing corporate resources for personal extravagances, and other ethical breaches. It took an indictment to finally humble him.

My observations reveal that narcissistic leaders view rules merely as nuisances, denying their selfish desires. Their arrogance breeds a predictable pattern. They will pursue self-interest in clear violation of rules, ignore advisor's warning of consequences, express defiance rather than remorse when transgressions come to light, force their ouster through escalating scandal, and leave behind a toxically individualistic culture in dire need of deep reforms.

This arrogance syndrome stems from profoundly distorted thinking. These leaders believe themselves special and above norms, assume rules do not apply to them, disregard risks in pursuit of glory, and reject criticism as motivated by envy or stupidity. Organizations must recognize the red flags of such narcissistic arrogance and intervene before it is too late. No leader is above the law or core values. Charismatic figures often mistake their ability to coerce compliance for actual authority. But in time, reality catches up. And the greater the heights, the steeper the fall.

One of the prime dangers of narcissistic leaders is their utter blindness to their own arrogance and misconduct. Convinced of their own superiority, they are unable to see the breaches of ethics and norms that should be red flags. But as outside observers, we must be vigilant for warning signs like openly criticizing policies, justifying unethical actions as acceptable for themselves, expressing disdain for oversight, and abusing power for personal gain.

With early intervention, mild narcissistic tendencies may be tempered before they escalate into full force behaviors. But once narcissism crosses a critical threshold, stringent regulation or even removal of the narcissistic leader may become necessary before they irreparably destroy the cultural foundations of ethics and morality within an organization. We must not wait for the inevitable fall to act. By then, the damage is done.

Surrounded by Yes-Men: How Narcissists Gain Power

A technology mogul prized loyalty above all else. He filled his board with yes-men who were amazed by his persona and would cater to his every need without question. Internal dysfunction was concealed beneath soaring revenues. But eventually, his uncontrolled narcissism drove the company toward ruin. Few dared confront the naked emperor. Narcissists gain power by attracting people who praise them. They reward flatterers and punish truth-tellers. This condones reckless egos upon organizations through:

- Craving loyalty tests rather than getting results. Narcissists desire praise, not progress.
- Building inner circles of devotees. Yes-men reflect the leader's distorted self-image.
- Eliminating nonconformists. Any criticism, even constructive, threatens their fragile egos.
- Excessive gratification. Narcissists feel entitled to extreme privileges and self-pleasure.

- Image obsession. PR and branding matter more than underlying performance.
- Exploiting organizational assets. The appropriate resources for personal vanity.

Enabling narcissistic leaders through blind loyalty does profound damage. Yes-men fosters corruption, instability, and unethical cultures. Leaders must surround themselves with wisdom and truth, not empty praise. As King Solomon wrote, "The one who flatters his neighbor spreads a net for his feet." (Proverbs 29:5)

Escaping this trap requires actively seeking critical counsel and empowering honesty from an inner circle with genuine independence and concern for institutional health above pleasing the powerful. There is a path out of darkness if narcissistic leaders have the courage to listen.

Chapter Summary:

- Narcissistic leaders cast long, dark shadows over the work culture. Their volatile egos and need for control breed fear and instability. Rationalizing unethical actions, they leave damaged organizations and bruised people in their wake.
- Though narcissists construct false outward confidence, fragile self-worth festers inside. They exploit people as instruments for ego goals, while their lack of empathy hollows out relationships. Understanding these rooted drivers gives insight into how they can be reformed.
- The burden of managing narcissistic dysfunction eventually takes an immense toll – subpar strategy, talent exodus, and culture toxicity. But with early diagnosis, oversight

constraints and accountability policies, organizations can mitigate harm.

- Mild narcissistic tendencies may improve, but engrained pathology may not be fixable. Protection depends on transparency, providing feedback channels, and rewarding ethics over self-interest. But prevention is a must - narcissists exploit trust.

- The central problem is that narcissists surround themselves with yes-men, endorsing their distorted self-image. But courageous leaders empower truth-tellers and seek out independent counsel focused on institutional health first.

Chapter 7 | The No-Common-Sense Leader

Examining the Lost Art of Logical Thinking

Common sense is a lost commodity in today's world, and it is also the foundation of sound leadership. To put it plainly, it is the ability to think logically using common sense rationale to make great decisions. It represents the basic logic, wisdom, and emotional intelligence required to make good judgments daily. While flashy leaders grab headlines, those grounded in practical wisdom build great organizations. Lacking common sense creates dysfunction. Leaders who complicate the simple or disregard the obvious sow confusion. Those devoid of "street smarts" struggle to relate to people. Common sense may appear boring, but abundant examples prove it indispensable.

What is Common Sense?

Common sense represents our inborn capacity for sound judgment and practical wisdom. It is the intuitive ability we all have to make good decisions using basic logic, filtered through the lens of real-world experience and emotional intelligence. You cannot learn common sense from a textbook – it is cultivated through living life and gaining perspective. It springs from having enough "street smarts" and maturity to simplify complexity, cut through noise and see obvious solutions that avoid over-thinking.

Common sense exposes foolish ideas that may sound clever but defy basic reasoning. It grasps subtle distinctions and understands how things play out in real human contexts, not just in theory. While common sense may seem unglamorous compared to high intelligence, it is the foundation of practical wisdom. Common sense allows ordinary people to make extraordinary judgments and decisions in all walks of life. It anchors leaders in reality and helps them relate to various perspectives.

Though underappreciated, common sense is the bedrock of sound leadership. It represents collective wisdom filtered through experience. While smarts come and go, common sense deepens over time - and leaders missing this key ingredient can bring about disaster. In an increasingly complex world, this commonsense wisdom is more vital than ever.

Why Common-Sense Matters

Leadership brings the heavy responsibility of making decisions that affect others. This duty requires sound judgment and sensible choices. Leaders lacking basic common sense will struggle to fulfill this responsibility wisely. Every judgment call relies on common sense - from major strategic decisions down to determining daily priorities. Clear thinking and clear communication are trademarks of effective leadership. Using complex language might impress some, but it often just confuses people. Practical solutions that make intuitive sense inspire belief in the leader's competence.

But when leaders lose touch with on-the-ground realities, it breeds dysfunction within teams. Lacking common sense distorts perceptions, creates blind spots, and leads to poor decisions with serious consequences. Leaders devoid of basic logic bring about disaster. That is why cultivating common sense is so crucial. Leaders must hone the ability to size up situations intuitively, filter out noise, and make choices anchored in reality, not theory. Life experience transfers practical wisdom over time. But leaders must also remain humble enough to keep learning as the world changes.

Common sense balances raw intellect's sharpness with the soft power of emotional intelligence. It allows leaders to simplify the complex, spot the obvious, and relate to all people. While underappreciated, common sense is the bedrock of sound leadership - and its absence guarantees failure.

The Risks of Needless Complexity

Some leaders have a tendency to make simple things sound more complex than they need to be. They use fancy jargon and complicated language in an attempt to seem intelligent. But this false sense of complexity just confuses colleagues and obscures common sense solutions, staring everyone in the face.

Using unnecessary, complex terms does not make a leader seem more profound. More often than not, it hides the fact that the leader himself is confused. The truth is often simple and elegant. True wisdom conveys even highly complex ideas in a clear and compelling way.

Steve Jobs exemplified this ability. The most brilliant leaders have a gift for simplicity and clarity, not complications and confusing language. They aim to simplify concepts rather than obscure them behind longwinded jargon.

Great judgment rests in a leader's ability to filter out noise and isolate the few critical signals that matter most. The functional leader eliminates needless complexity in favor of well-designed simplicity. They understand that restraint often conveys wisdom far better than showing off vocabulary.

At the end of the day, practical common sense must anchor complex ideas in reality. The savvy leader strives for crystal-clear communication and intuitive solutions that feel almost effortless. Anything else risks becoming lost in abstract ideas and untethered from common sense.

The Limits of Book Smarts

Common sense comes from practical life experience. It represents instincts and gut-level intuitions that cannot be learned from textbooks. When leaders get too caught up in abstract theories, they risk losing touch with on-the-ground realities.

We've all seen brilliant thinkers who lack basic emotional intelligence and "street smarts." But leadership is not an academic exercise - it requires understanding and motivating diverse people day to day. Relying too much on book knowledge while lacking real-world experience creates blind spots and leadership limitations. Without enough "street smarts," dysfunctional leaders will struggle to relate to and inspire their teams.

Raw intellect clearly matters, but it isn't sufficient. The savviest leaders balance academic knowledge with street smarts gained from rich life experience. They combine high EQ and IQ. This enables them to connect with, motivate, and lead others effectively. At the end of the day, leadership relies more on practical wisdom than abstract intelligence. The most brilliant leaders are grounded in the realities of human experience--which textbooks simply can't teach.

Missing the Obvious

Some common leadership pitfalls like overthinking and analysis paralysis cause even the smartest leaders to miss obvious solutions. Overthinking everything leads to making big assumptions based on very little real evidence. It also makes leaders fail to notice meaningful patterns or understand the subtle differences in situations. This distorted thinking overrides basic logic and intuition.

Good judgment relies just as much on practical intuition and mental shortcuts as rigorous logic. The most effective leaders make sound calls by artfully balancing both. They avoid the trap of needlessly complicating routine decisions that could be dealt with simply. And they have the courage to take simple, decisive actions, not just complex ones.

Clarity of vision flows from clarity of thought grounded in lived experiences. The functional leader distinguishes meaningless noise from deceptively simple signals. By mastering the art of simplicity, they bring focus to complexity. But overthinking breeds confusion, obscuring the obvious. At the end of the day, common sense must anchor intellect in reality. The savviest leaders blend razor-sharp analysis with street-tested intuition. This allows them to see both the forest and the trees clearly.

When Everyone Just Agrees

When leaders surround themselves only with people who agree with them, they can easily lose perspective. They get stuck in echo chambers where no one questions their assumptions or offers opposing views. Without the bravery to have open and transparent debates about ideas, leaders start to think in narrow-minded ways. They just go along with whatever dominant narrative the group holds, breeding conformity.

To stay realistic, leaders need to actively seek out and listen to people who will challenge their own views, not just validate them. The wise leader intentionally gives a voice to thoughtful people who disagree with them. This breaks the curse of groupthink by injecting different perspectives and new possibilities into the conversation.

Sound judgment demands exploring all credible evidence objectively, not just data that fits one's worldview. Getting regular input from people with very different opinions protects leaders against distorted views of reality that are warped by listening only to those who are similar to them. By humbly seeking truth in the form of disagreement as well as consent, leaders widen their horizons and strengthen their ability to make balanced calls. The fruits of diversity in viewpoints and debate lead to wiser decisions, not weakness.

Losing Touch with the Front Lines

Functional leadership demands connecting with ground-level realities. But the higher leaders rise in organizations, the more removed they often become from everyday frontline experiences. Sheltered in executive suites and affluence, top leaders can forget what life looks like for the average employee or customer. Without regular frontline interactions, leaders progressively lose touch with the real challenges and constraints that employees face daily. The most effective leaders make a point to stay closely connected with field operations and frontline workers. They make time to solicit unfiltered insights from the front lines that provide valuable perspective and understanding.

But with success, ego and arrogance naturally creep in at times. Leaders get comfortable in the C-suite and lose their hunger for foundational information. However, staying humble and eager to keep learning from all levels of the organization can balance out this dangerous tendency toward narrow-mindedness and ignorance of ground realities. By making an effort to get into the field and listen with humility, leaders can retain the common sense that comes from contact with raw experience. This regular infusion of perspective protects them against the executive disease of isolation and pride that eventually infects many long-tenured leaders over time.

The Hard Fall of the No Common Sense Leader

History shows many gifted leaders suffered dramatic downfalls due to astonishing lapses in common sense. Arrogance blinded them to obvious risks and realities right in front of them. They lacked advisors willing to challenge faulty thinking rooted in pride rather than reason.

For example, President Nixon's arrogance led to illegal abuses of power, despite clear warnings from staff. His lack of common sense destroyed a successful political career. In business, Lehman Brothers CEO Dick Fuld's ego drove reckless risk-taking, ignoring clear signs of impending financial disaster.

His absence of wise, common-sense counsel enabled blindness that culminated in the firm's catastrophic collapse during the 2008 crisis.

Across arenas, the paradoxical rise-and-fall leadership cycle repeats when common sense judgment fails. Politicians brought down by trivial scandals. Visionary founders who drive thriving companies into the ground through ego-driven overreach. Millionaire celebrities jailed for petty theft. When common sense lapses, leaders inevitably overestimate their ability and invite disaster.

Thus, the functional leader stays grounded in reality, logic and humility - not ego. By valuing diverse perspectives, making decisions rationally, and avoiding arrogance's temptations, they maintain sound judgment over time, avoiding the mistakes of so many gifted but tragically flawed predecessors. History provides warnings to guide us - if we remain open and vigilant.

Cultivating Common Sense

How can leaders strengthen and cultivate common sense over time? First, by proactively raising self-awareness of blind spots. Regularly seeking critical feedback provides perspective and protects against distortions. Remaining open and humble, with a hunger for input from diverse viewpoints, is crucial, too.

Leaders must also stay closely connected to frontline realities through direct interactions with the field. This builds emotional intelligence and battle-tested intuition at the ground level. They need the courage to simplify complex issues to their essence and avoid groupthink by thinking independently.

Finally, common sense expands through broad life experience over time. The more exposed leaders are to different worlds and challenges, the more practical wisdom they internalize. Hard-won lessons gained through years of experience and mistakes gradually embed within leaders, shaping resilient judgment and mastery. At its core, functional leadership requires deep practical wisdom and maturity, not just raw intellect. Common sense represents this hard-earned capacity to simplify complexities, spot the obvious, and discern differences in relatable ways. It anchors leaders in reality.

Leaders lacking basic logic, emotional intelligence, and life experience court disaster. But humility, diverse input, and the courage to think independently cultivate common sense and wisdom despite blind spots. May we have the humility to learn these essential lessons before experience teaches us the hard way.

Chapter Summary:

- Common sense represents the intuitive capacity for sound judgment filtered through real-world experience. It simplifies complexity, grasps subtlety, and anchors leaders in reality. But many lack this practical wisdom.

- Leadership demands decisions grounded in basic logic and street smarts. Without common sense, leaders breed dysfunction through poor judgment, blindness, and disjointed actions. But experience aids in this intuitive mastery over time.

- Even the most brilliant minds outsmart themselves through excessive complexity. True wisdom conveys the profound with simplicity and restraint. Great leaders distinguish meaningless noise from deceptively simple truths.

- Narrow-minded echo chambers warp perspective. By humbly seeking diverse views, leaders gain immunity against distorted realities. Truth emerges through fostering candid debate across differences, not suppressing contrary views.

- Regular frontline interactions safeguard leaders against losing touch as they rise. But unchecked ego threatens clarity. Staying humble, rational, and self-aware preserves common sense against pride's corruption. Our blind spots obscure the obvious. History warns us if we have ears to hear

Chapter 8 | The Passive Leader

Evaluation of Docile, Conflict-Averse Leaders Who Avoid Difficult Decisions

My research reveals that few dysfunctional leadership traits wreak more havoc than passivity. Passive leaders avoid hard decisions, dodge direct dialogue, and shun accountability. Though seemingly conflict-averse, their inactivity breeds disorder. Avoiding messy realities lets problems fester unseen, eroding trust, and performance. But hope remains. With moral courage, those paralyzed by indecision can yet become empowered to lead. By converting good intentions into bold stewardship, passive leaders can ignite cultural renewal. The path requires conquering fears of criticism and change. But transforming from passive to proactive liberates enormous potential in people and organizations.

In this chapter, we'll examine the different forms of passive leadership and their cascading impacts. Understanding the root psychology behind conflict avoidance positions us to guide passive leaders toward living their values with moral action. For both people and organizations to thrive, leaders must convert good intentions into courageous stewardship.

The High Price of Avoiding Problems

Early in my career, I heard about a nonprofit leader who ignored serious issues despite employees sounding alarms. He avoided addressing poor performance, missed deadlines, bullying behaviors and more. Instead, he joked about conflicts and urged people to "get along." By denying dysfunction, he allowed minor problems to become existential threats. Passive leaders regulate anxiety through blindness rather than facing difficulties. This "see no evil, hear no evil" approach distorts optimism while reflecting deep pessimism about improving situations. Feeling unable to make things better leads to giving up or focusing on less important things. Nothing will crush a good employee's spirit faster than watching their boss tolerate a bad employee.

But real hope emerges from faith in human potential and the moral courage to cultivate it. As Vaclav Havel wrote, "Hope is not the conviction that something will turn out well but the certainty that something is worth doing no matter how it turns out." Leaders need to find the strength to confront challenges. Avoidance only compounds them.

The Perils of Indecisive Leadership

There was an executive paralyzed with indecision about which marketing proposal to fund, afraid of making the wrong choice. He hesitated, asked for more data, and stuck with what he already knew rather than trying new creative partnerships. His inaction stifled growth as people waited endlessly for direction.

Passive leaders have difficulty moving forward when things are unclear. Seeking total certainty breeds analysis paralysis and rationalized procrastination. But obsessing over potential missteps also guarantees no forward movement. As Lao Tzu wrote, a journey of a thousand miles begins with a single step.

Progress emerges through imperfect action, repetition and growth, not endlessly waiting for the perfect moment.

Courage arises from acting despite fear. Functional leaders develop trust in their judgement through experience, not a certainty. Decisions can be prone to human error, and still far better than no choice at all. Indecisiveness breeds organizational atrophy. The consistent forward movement, however flawed, builds momentum.

The Dangers of Mistaking Kindness for Weakness

Many well-intentioned, nurturing leaders mistakenly equate kindness with conflict avoidance. Unwilling to upset people, they shy away from direct feedback and addressing problems head-on. By over-emphasizing positivity and praise over accountability, they allow mediocrity to fester. While rooted in caring intentions, this passive approach breeds entitlement and erodes excellence. In their reluctance to have candid conversations, such leaders fail to provide the clarity, consequences, and growth opportunities that would actually support team members' potential.

True kindness requires courage – the willingness to address problems using practical examples directly and compassionately. It means balancing praise for progress with candid feedback about poor choices. This growth-oriented candor elevates teams far more than empty clichés ever could.

There is an upside when leaders move past personal discomfort to foster excellence in others. As Henry Ford noted, "My best friend is the one who brings out the best in me." Stewarding talent demands caring enough to be honest, not just being polite. The path of courage and candor, though difficult, holds the greatest hope for a positive impact.

The Dangers of Tolerating Unethical Actions

Passive leaders often prioritize personal comfort over character and principles. In their conflict avoidance, they remain silent and tolerate unethical actions, dishonesty, or mistreatment even when they know it is wrong. But through acceptance and unwillingness to intervene, they enable harm and become complicit in its continuation. As Edmund Burke wrote, "The only thing necessary for the triumph of evil is for good men to do nothing."

It takes great humility for passive leaders to accept they may allow wrongs to occur through inaction. And even greater courage to finally confront such unethical behaviors directly, with care rather than judgment. There is real hope for cultural healing when passive leaders find the will to move from bystanders to proactive defenders of ethics and human dignity.

The path of courage calls us to stand for something larger than ourselves. Through boldly speaking truth despite fear, passive leaders can rediscover moral purpose. Even late interventions plant integrity seeds that may gradually transform cultures over time. But passivity must give way to principled leadership, or both people and principles will perish.

Cultivating Courage Over Passivity

Transforming passivity requires self-honesty about root causes like conflict avoidance, pessimism, and apathy. Then courage builds gradually. As the Serenity Prayer says, we gain wisdom by recognizing our power to shape some circumstances, accept what we cannot change, and pursue growth.

Leaders must believe people and conditions can improve through effort. Progress emerges from perseverance. Character is measured by whether we show up in hard times, not just easy ones. There is a path from passive mindsets breeding dysfunction to proactive leadership cultivating potential.

With bravery and support, passive leaders can become champions who provide direction, accountability, and hope grounded in reality. But fear-based avoidance only worsens problems and erodes morality over time. I remain ever hopeful about human potential. But passivity must first be surrendered, or it spreads like slow poison – limiting possibilities, lowering standards, and breeding distrust in people's capabilities. This high cost demands courageous action.

The Virtuous Cycle of Proactive Leadership

The ultimate irony of passivity is that avoiding feared situations only hands more power over to others. But courageous action transforms what we fear. Proactive leaders face difficulties directly. They support team members with care and candid feedback. By imposing fair consequences, they reinforce shared values. Courage establishes trust and a healthy culture, which empowers teams to excel.

Excellence then attracts talent and investments, fueling sustainable growth. Growth enables bolder vision and purpose. And so, this creates a positive virtuous cycle. While passivity becomes a self-fulfilling prophecy, proactive leadership creates self-sustaining momentum. This upward spiral requires humility to admit uncertainty, exercise imperfect judgment, and learn from errors. But real hope springs from faith in human potential for growth. Leaders must hold fast to this moral vision and have the courage to act upon it.

There will always be a natural fear of making hard decisions. But distinguishing destructive distress from healthy trouble is wisdom. As President FDR said during dark times, "The only thing we have to fear is fear itself." False comfort breeds complacency, while dread spurs diligence. Some anxiety guards what we care about most. Proactive leaders leverage self-doubt as an asset for continual improvement, not as an excuse for paralysis. Hard decisions clarify values, strengthen teams, and move organizations forward. Courage is a muscle that grows through exercise. And giving up passivity opens up opportunities to take the right action instead.

Leading With Moral Courage

In many ways, leadership is simply moral courage made visible through actions. It means standing for values and making difficult but necessary decisions out of duty, not comfort. Courage questions old assumptions, challenges biases, and illuminates inconvenient truths. It drives leaders to do the right thing for others instead of what benefits themselves. And it gives voice to those made silent through fear.

But moral courage also requires exercising power with great compassion. Functional leadership calls on us to lean into discomfort and manage conflicts while seeing humanity's larger potential, even in those causing harm. Leaders also need confidence that their small actions can add up to significant change over time. Progress depends on perseverance.

These are the universal truths that all leaders need to commit to each day. Though moral courage feels scarce amidst uncertainty, it arises from acting out of hope, not fear. This is leadership's great calling. On this challenging but hopeful path, may we find strength in fellowship and purpose greater than ourselves. And may we answer fear with wisdom and passivity with action. The thresholds we least want to cross often lead to the most meaningful growth.

Chapter Summary:

- Passive leaders avoid hard decisions and accountability, but their conflict avoidance breeds dysfunction. By denying problems, they allow preventable threats to compound. Courage addresses difficulties early before they escalate.

- Passive leaders endlessly hesitate without acting for fear of imperfection. Paralysis breeds atrophy while consistent forward movement, however flawed, gathers momentum. With wisdom and experience, courage arises to act despite uncertainty.

- Many caring leaders mistake passivity for kindness. But problems fester without candid clarity and consequences. True kindness combines uncompromising standards with empathy, support, and constructive criticism to foster growth.

- Tolerating unethical actions makes leaders complicit through acceptance. Speaking truth to power and upholding integrity renews moral purpose, though difficult. Even belated actions can gradually improve culture.

- With self-honesty and perseverance, passive leaders gain courage through moral education, encouragement, and small brave steps. Their renewed leadership establishes trust and excellence. This turns the negative momentum into a positive, self-reinforcing loop.

Chapter 9 | The Unethical Leader

Rule-Breaking, Dishonesty, and Illegal Behavior by Leaders

Now, let me take you on a journey through the treacherous terrain of leadership and ethics. It's a topic close to my heart because I have witnessed, time and again, how integrity lies at the very core of great leadership. Leadership is an immense privilege that amplifies our human vulnerabilities--fear, greed, desperation. Without self-awareness, even well-intentioned leaders risk ethical missteps when faced with deception's temptation. I want to shed some light on the shadows that leaders often find themselves entangled in--the world of lies, cheating, and deceit.

Now, you might wonder, "Why would leaders, who often start with noble intentions, get caught up in this web of unethical behavior?" It's a valid question, and the answer lies in the subtle attraction of compromise. As leaders, we are driven by a desire to succeed, to achieve our goals, and sometimes, we might convince ourselves that a little bending of the rules is justifiable for the greater good. But that is where the slippery slope begins. These actions, born from good intentions or not, have a devastating impact. They erode trust within our teams, creating an environment poisoned by deception. Trust is the currency of leadership, and without it, our influence decreases.

In this chapter, we will shed light on the psychological and cultural forces that corrode the moral fabric within organizations. We will explore those treacherous slopes that lead us towards rule-breaking, and we will shine a light on the cultural factors and human motivations that often push us in that direction. You see, it's not always a black-and-white scenario. Understanding the roots of unethical behavior is the first step toward redemption through courage, honesty, and renewal of values.

But what if the damage has already been done? Trust has been shattered, and the path back to integrity seems burdened with obstacles. Well, that is where moral courage comes into play. Rebuilding trust requires a steadfast commitment to doing what is right, even when it is tough.

Systemic change is often necessary, too. Sometimes, the very culture of an organization encourages unethical behavior. As leaders, we must be the change agents, setting the tone and expectations for our teams. We lead by example, showing that our actions align with our values.

I know it is not an easy journey but there is hope for renewal. When our values align with our actions, we can rebuild that trust. So, let us embark on this quest to understand the pitfalls, recognize the signs, and be the leaders who restore integrity and inspire others to follow suit. Remember, with integrity as your compass, you'll always find your way.

Eroding Integrity: The Spread of Lies

It often starts gradually--a distorted truth here, a concealed loss there. But deception builds on itself. Early compromises make it easier to tell bigger lies later. Soon, dishonesty becomes reflexive rather than deliberate.

What motivates respected leaders to take this treacherous path? The root causes are universal human weaknesses - fear of losing status, greed for power and riches, desperation to hide mistakes. Fearful leaders exaggerate success to protect their egos. Greedy leaders see ethics as obstacles to personal gain. Desperate leaders hide failures when overwhelmed by pressure.

But as philosopher Ralph Waldo Emerson observed, "Every lie is a kind of suicide for the liar." Lies drain relationships of trust, which is leadership's lifeblood. They sow anxiety and corrode organizational culture from within. When exposed, lies amplify feelings of betrayal among stakeholders. Any immediate gains are outweighed by long-term damage to one's reputation.

I often advise leaders who face deception's temptation to pause and consider the long-term consequences. Lies may temporarily obscure failure, but they also cloud success. Because influence depends on integrity, surrendering it for any reason betrays leadership itself. Those who take this fateful step risk losing all moral authority.

The Slippery Slope of Fraud

Even principled executives can gradually slide down the slippery slope of financial deception. Once, a CEO was charged with fraud and he began rebuilding trust after it destroyed their predecessor company. Despite new financial controls, some struggling managers facing extreme pressure rationalized "minor" accounting manipulation as justifiable for the greater good. But artificially inflating performance numbers, even slightly, distorts reality. Leaders lose sight of true strengths and weaknesses. Poor decisions snowball until disaster strikes, as it happened here. Meanwhile, fraud corrodes culture and morale from the inside like cancer.

Warning signs I teach leaders to watch for include discrepancies in financial reports, murky affiliate transactions, rapid revenue recognition, and resistance to audits or controls. But fraud often advances unseen. That is why culture is so crucial--ethics and integrity training must start early, long before threats arise. And once uncovered, fraud demands total transparency--firing offenders, fully cooperating with investigations, and overhauling broken systems. This path of radical openness feels excruciating but ultimately cleanses. Only a culture rebuilt on a moral example from the top can restore trust.

The Poisoned Fruit of Prejudice

Unconscious bias and double standards among leaders breed unhealthy cultures over time. There once was an elected official known for demeaning female employees through sexist language and harassment. Oblivious to his own prejudice, he viewed himself as their friend. But his actions signaled to the entire organization that women were inferior. Many talented employees left rather than endure such humiliations. Those who remained suffered silently, too intimidated to speak out. By letting prejudice exclude people, this leader hurt his team and let down people relying on him.

Addressing systemic bias requires moving beyond policies to fundamentally transform culture through moral education, self-reflection, and courageously confronting harsh realities before authentic healing can occur. Lasting change is built through championing reasonable systems not reacting to isolated incidents. Though long and challenging, this work of honoring human dignity holds the power to redeem broken cultures.

The Façade of Virtue

There was a CEO publicly devoted to ethics and corporate social responsibility. But behind closed doors, he dismissed these principles as mere public relations, believing profits matter above all. He freely engaged in bribery and silenced internal opposition. Stakeholders felt betrayed when his deceitfulness emerged.

Leaders who glorify values externally while secretly disregarding them internally breed skepticism through hypocrisy. Their mixed messages distort cultures. As their facades of virtue crumble, morale and motivation collapse. Employees begin mirroring the unethical behaviors leaders denounce publicly but silently encourage through their own actions.

Such leaders poison organizations from within while inflicting external reputational damage. After ethical failures, truly fixing trust means taking accountability - admitting hard truths, aligning words with actions and engaging others to strengthen values and transparency. Leaders must act with integrity themselves if they want to require ethical behavior from others. Demanding morality without modeling it will seem hollow and hypocritical.

The Redemption of Moral Courage

Functional leadership means occupying the lonely post of the moral frontline, guided solely by inner values. But redemption remains possible even when integrity lapses. As Solzhenitsyn wrote, good and evil pass through every heart. Even the Bible says that we all have sinned and fallen short of the glory of God (Romans 3:23). By courageously confronting our own darkness, we light the way for others.

Progress depends not on perfection but on persistence in striving toward truth and justice despite setbacks. Though difficult, this journey of moral renewal renews integrity's foundation. Leadership is a lifelong process of self-examination, growth, and stewardship of culture.

Illuminating the Shadows

Leaders without integrity inflict generational damage upon cultures. But transformation occurs when leaders look inward with humility and embark on the difficult path of renewal in service of a higher purpose.

This journey requires surrendering the illusion's comfort to reality's harsh light. It demands rigorous self-examination and moral discipline against fear, greed, pride, and other inner demons. The path challenges leaders to align words with actions, even at great personal cost.

Walking this narrow road can feel lonesome. But by illuminating darkness within themselves, enlightened leaders light the way for others. Their renewed moral authority builds cultures of purpose, fulfillment, and shared humanity.

Progress will be gradual, punctuated by stumbles as moral muscle is rebuilt. But persistence and transparency in examining one's shortcomings transform organizations, even amid occasional setbacks. By passing through the fire of self-reckoning and allowing it to forge wisdom, honesty, and justice within, leaders emerge renewed as ethical role models.

After decades of studying leadership's ethical journeys, I share these reflections. Universal human flaws ensure we will all stumble at times. But how we respond defines us. Each failure, if met with courage, humility, and moral vigor, carries hope for leadership's rebirth. The path is difficult but necessary.

Chapter Summary:

- Deception tempts even ethical leaders through early compromises that pave the way for larger lies. But truth-telling defines leadership. Lies erode trust and cloud judgment. Stopping to consider results first keeps a leader's integrity intact.

- Even principled executives rationalize "minor" fraud under pressure, distorting realities. Warning signs include financial discrepancies and resistance to transparency. But cultural safeguards like ethics training and accountability prevent this ethical erosion and allow trust restoration after failures.

- Unconscious bias breeds unhealthy, exclusive cultures over time through prejudice and double standards. Promoting systemic fairness and confronting harsh realities holds power to redeem divided people. But authentic change requires self-examination, moral education, and courage.

- Leaders who glorify values while secretly disregarding them spread skepticism through hypocrisy. But integrity aligns words with actions. It requires admitting hard truths and strengthening transparency. Therein reputations and cultures are renewed through steadfast commitment to morality.

- Though all stumble, redemption remains possible through spiritual courage and growth. By illuminating our inner shadows with honesty, we light the way for others. Progress flows from perseverance and self-examination, not perfection.

SECTION TWO

Chapter 10 | Dysfunctional by Association

How Toxic Environments Turn Good Leaders Bad

Throughout my career, I have seen even the most principled and capable leaders become dysfunctional unintentionally when immersed in toxicity for too long. Like pollution clouding the sky and dimming the sun, no inner light stays bright when surrounded by cultural darkness day after day.

This sobering reality highlights the immense situational and systemic forces that can erode the character of even the best among us over time. While personal responsibility certainly matters, dismissing struggling leaders as merely "bad apples" discounts outside influences infecting their integrity. By taking a more subtle view and examining how dysfunctional environments contaminate good people gradually, we gain wisdom to strengthen and support one another through difficulty.

The Insidious Spread of Toxicity

Once, there was a Fortune 500 company that boasted a remarkably ethical culture for decades. Employees took pride in its values-driven reputation. But a new CEO came in seeking rapid growth at any cost. Profit became prioritized over purpose as toxic behaviors were normalized from the top. Seasoned leaders, once known for their character, made gradual compromises to meet unrealistic targets in the ruthless new climate. In their drive to meet unrealistic targets, they adopted the same unhealthy habits they likely once deplored. It was a cautionary case study of how cultural dysfunction can spread.

The research shows predictable patterns in how even highly principled leaders adopt the same dysfunctional behaviors they deplore when immersed in toxicity long enough. External pressures mount as growth stalls and circumstances grow more challenging. Negative coping mechanisms form as exhausted leaders lash out under stress or become withdrawn. Conduct gets internally rationalized as serving the greater cause despite personal misgivings. And dysfunction becomes inevitable as individual character buckles under the weight of cultural corruption.

Without intervention, once solid leaders gradually continue the dysfunction they inherit. However, courageous cultures can provide support through restorative interventions before it's too late if they have the moral willpower to do so. None can thrive in isolation for long. As the legend Alexander the Great said, "I am dying with the help of too many physicians." Even the mightiest need periodic healing, restoration, and course corrections when they are veering far off track.

By recognizing the insidious spread of toxicity, we come closer to solutions. Establishing guardrails and introducing self-awareness helps inoculate even strong individuals against gradual demoralization. While situational pressures persist, developing wisdom and communal support systems can bolster people to withstand corrosion, make amends, and write new chapters. But intervention must come soon, or all is lost.

Corruption Through Conformity

Corruption through conformity is a phenomenon in which people engage in unethical or corrupt behavior because they see others doing it and believe that it is the expected or accepted behavior. This can happen in any setting, but it is more likely to occur in cultures where corruption is widespread and tolerated.

In the example that I used earlier, the Wells Fargo executive is a classic case of corruption through conformity. The executive initially resisted opening fraudulent accounts, but he eventually gave in to the pressure from his superiors and colleagues. He saw that others were doing it and he didn't want to be singled out or punished.

When unethical behaviors go unchallenged, it sends the message that it is acceptable to make light of serious matters. When lapses by superiors are overlooked, it sends the message that they are not held to the same standards as everyone else. When whistleblowers are ostracized, it sends the message that speaking out against corruption is not tolerated. And when success depends on violating "unwritten rules," it sends the message that the ends justify the means.

It is important to remember that corruption is not always a conscious choice. Many people who engage in corrupt behavior do so because they feel like they have no other choice. They may be afraid of retaliation, they may want to fit in, or they may simply not know that their behavior is wrong. That's why it is important to create positive cultures that discourage corruption. This means creating cultures where people feel comfortable speaking up against unethical behavior, where there are clear consequences for corruption, and where everyone is held to the same standards.

It is also important to remember that we are all susceptible to corruption through conformity. We all want to fit in and be accepted, and we may be tempted to rationalize our behavior if we see others doing it. That's why it is important to be aware of the signs of corruption and to speak up when we see it happening. Here are some things you can do to help prevent corruption through conformity:

Challenge unethical behavior. If you see someone engaging in unethical behavior, don't be afraid to speak up. Let them know that their behavior is wrong and that you won't tolerate it.

Support whistleblowers. Whistleblowers are people who speak out against corruption. They often face retaliation, but it is important to support them. Let them know that you believe them and that you are there for them.

Create a culture of integrity. This means creating a culture where people feel comfortable speaking up against unethical behavior, where there are clear consequences for corruption, and where everyone is held to the same standards.

By doing these things, we can help to create a world where corruption is not tolerated and where everyone can thrive.

Burnout: When Functional Becomes Dysfunctional

In the past, I once had the privilege of working for an organization with an incredibly healthy work culture, where morale soared high. It was a place where employees genuinely loved their work, myself included. With my successful experience in leading teams, I was honored to be promoted to a director-level role. However, a fateful mistake occurred when upper-level leadership failed to backfill my prior position after my promotion. Consequently, I found myself shouldering the responsibilities of both my old and new roles--an unsustainable burden.

As the plates began spinning faster, I quickly realized there simply were not enough hours in the day to keep them all moving. But in my devotion to the organization's mission, I viewed this Herculean effort as a testament to my dedication. I worked tirelessly, striving to hold everything together while refusing to show any outward signs of weakness. Eventually, I mustered the courage to explicitly warn my oversight about the situation, fully aware of the budget constraints we faced. Unfortunately, the solutions offered were limited. Gradually, the plates began to topple, one by one, and the mental and emotional toll mounted heavily on me.

Despite my repeated pleas for help, leadership failed to provide a viable solution for my unsustainable workload and emotional fatigue. The relentless demands of my dual role, coupled with the mounting pressure to deliver excellent results, led me to burnout and mental exhaustion. My once-stellar performance diminished sharply, and I went from being a highly functional leader to barely keeping my head above water. Disheartened and battle worn, I was relieved when the broken system ended up laying me off along with many staff and faculty. I felt let down by the very organization I had once held in such high regard. I had become the type of dysfunctional, ineffective leader that I deplored.

This tragedy repeats itself too often, as devotion without intervention depletes the most committed workers. Without support, their strengths morph into glaring weaknesses. The inverted characteristics of burned-out leaders can include:

- Confidence warping into anxiety, anger, and desperation
- Passion turning into detachment and pessimism
- Striving driving exhaustion and lapses in judgment

Promoting people without proper resources breeds discouragement. But self-awareness helps leaders manage their own vulnerabilities wisely. There is hope for renewal if exhaustion is addressed early before strengths turn to liabilities. Sustaining servant leadership over the long haul requires caring for the caregiver. Even the most devoted eventually burn out when giving from an empty vessel.

After a sabbatical and a new position, I eventually regained strength by training others to share burdens and speaking openly about burnout. But I learned the hard way that no amount of skill or good intent outweighs self-care. Grace and support sustain functional leadership over the long haul.

Chapter Summary:

- Even principled leaders gradually adopt dysfunctional behaviors when immersed in toxicity. External pressures and demoralization erode individual character over time. But courageous cultures can intervene before it becomes too late - with moral education, boundaries, and communal support.
- Cultures tolerate unethical behaviors by rationalizing them, signaling they are acceptable. This conformity corruption causes people to mirror misconduct. But positive cultures encourage speaking up against violations, upholding consistent standards and ethics at all levels.
- Leaders who preach values but don't follow them themselves are setting a bad example. This can lead to

people losing trust in leaders and institutions. When people say one thing but do another, it can lead to cynicism and a decline in moral standards. However, if we live up to our values and are honest about our shortcomings, we can rebuild our culture. This means admitting things that are difficult to hear and being transparent about our actions.

- Though all stumble at times, redemption remains possible through spiritual courage and growth. By illuminating our inner shadows with honesty, we light the way for others. Progress flows from perseverance and self-reckoning, not perfection.

- Without intervention, passionate leaders slip into dysfunction under overwhelming demands. But boundaries prevent depletion and sustain servant leadership over the long haul. When people are kind and supportive, it helps their strengths to grow and last. This is better than strengths turning into weaknesses, which can make society worse.

Chapter 11 | The Dysfunctional Work Culture

How Bad Leadership Infects Organizations and Creates Dysfunctional Environments

Over the years, I have personally seen the immense damage just one toxic leader at the top can inflict on a work culture. Like cancer, negative behaviors spread covertly until the entire organization is corrupted. Toxic leaders can operate through fear, deception, and abuse of power. They deliberately manipulate cultural dynamics to normalize dysfunction until ethical erosion reaches the core. Followers feel pressured to abandon their own values and mirror unethical behaviors modeled at the top.

In this chapter, we'll explore how toxic influence spreads through groups and early warning signs to spot. Understanding these cultural dynamics is key. Environments nurtured by wisdom, integrity, and care have the potential to positively influence struggling leaders. However, cultures poisoned by toxicity corrupt even otherwise ethical people over time through compromised standards, incentives, and modeling.

The Power of Context

Context and environment profoundly impact human behavior, for better or worse. While personal values matter, situational influences can override individual morality. That is why establishing a culture at the top can be so dangerous.

Unethical leaders infect organizations covertly by gradually seducing followers to compromise, telling themselves it is justified or necessary for survival. Small steps that go against what you believe in can make it easier to do bigger wrong things until what was wrong feels normal. People ultimately abandon moral codes under group pressure and rationalization.

But the opposite also holds promise. Cultures cultivated by moral leaders elevate standards through wisdom, care, and accountability. Within healthy work environments, people gain the courage to stand up to external unethical forces. That is why cultural stewardship represents leadership's highest calling. Both people and organizations remain vulnerable when integrity foundations erode.

Rotten Apples Spoil the Whole Bunch: The Spread of Dysfunction

Individual leaders profoundly shape organizational environments through their behaviors, which model standards for others consciously or unconsciously. When a toxic leader acts out, their dysfunctional conduct becomes normalized and spreads in a subtle way, like a rotten apple spoiling the whole bunch.

Even as some may be initially repelled, the warped reality of the toxic leader gradually becomes the cultural water everyone swims in if left unchecked. Past power abuses rewrite the playbooks for successors seeking to rise in the organization. Voices of opposition struggle to change such ingrained streams single-handedly.

Intervening requires raising consciousness among other organizational members before these dysfunctional patterns fully harden. As Margaret Mead said, "Never doubt that a small group of thoughtful, committed citizens can change the world; indeed, it's the only thing that ever has." Therein lies hope – engaging courageous allies early on to interrupt cycles of toxicity before they fully set. However, without intervention, "bad apple" leaders will infect others through their modeling of dysfunctional behaviors. Their distortions become slowly accepted, perpetuating harm across groups. The stakes are high in addressing root causes before it is too late.

Rules for Thee, But Not for Me: Hypocrisy at the Top

When leaders exempt themselves from organizational rules and codes of conduct, it signals to others that these standards only apply to lesser members of the group. Hypocrisy at the top breeds conflict, lack of concern, and skepticism. People feel like fools for investing in shared values that leaders undermine through their own deceitful actions. It evokes deep feelings of betrayal when revered authorities are revealed to be frauds.

Restoring lost trust in such situations requires authenticity and integrity from leaders. As Ralph Waldo Emerson wrote, "What you do speaks so loudly that I cannot hear what you say." Leaders must embody the values they embrace through their actions. The moral example holds far more power than hollow programs or policies alone.

Therein lies the only foundation upon which ethical cultures can truly flourish - through leaders who walk the talk consistently according to their principles. When words and deeds align, followers become inspired. But hypocrisy corrodes influence, leaving a void of distrust. The damage often cannot be undone.

Pressure Cookers: The Perils of Hyper-Competition

Leaders who deliberately pit followers against each other in hyper-competitive cultures fuel tremendous stress and paranoia rather than driving motivation and excellence. These combative, backstabbing climates force people to act in ruthless self-interest, cutting corners ethically and losing natural motivation. Over time, alienation increases and morale plummets as workers feel isolated, fending for themselves. Research shows that psychologically safe environments allowing colleagues to openly share knowledge and support each other's growth yield far superior results.

As Ray Dalio, founder of Bridgewater Associates, wrote, "Teamwork produces exponentially better results than individual performers." There is a key advantage in cultivating collaborative cultures focused on collective growth rather than individual glory.

But leaders who impose negative competition internally risk destroying cultural foundations. Some may call it "Darwinian" strength, but in reality, hyper-competitiveness breeds unethical behavior and human misery, corroding the organization from within. Wisdom cautions against stoking these counterproductive instincts.

Cubicle Farms: Depressing Work Environments

Too often, efficiency is prioritized over humanity in designing workplace environments. But the physical spaces leaders craft profoundly shape psychological experiences for employees. Impersonal, cramped, windowless cubicle farms bathed in harsh fluorescent lighting breed depression, dread, and despair. Depriving workspaces crush motivation and performance over time, no matter the nature of the work. Human beings need dignity and thriving conditions to excel.

However, thoughtfully human-centered offices factoring in natural light, greenery, ergonomic furniture, collaborative zones, and personalization cultivate creativity and morale. As Winston Churchill said, "We shape our buildings; thereafter, they shape us." As functional leaders, we are to craft workplaces that uplift the human spirit, not crushing it.

The costs of oppressive work environments are real. No culture can flourish in depressing "fields of despair" where people feel stripped of value and empowerment. But with care, the right infrastructure can empower potential.

Spotting Toxic Cultures Early

While extreme cases manifest clearly, cultural toxicity often grows rapidly through subtle undercurrents requiring vigilance to detect:

- Us vs. them mentalities breeding tribalism and fear of conflict
- Echo chambers valuing loyalty over honesty
- Power imbalances enable abuses that get normalized
- Victim blaming when people report misconduct
- Focus on image over underlying practices
- Lack of transparency and oversight framework
- Tolerance of unethical behavior that serves short-term interests

When people in power start cutting small corners or bending the rules, it can quickly spiral out of control if no one intervenes early. Small ethical compromises made out of expediency often compound into larger and more brazen abuses over time. Gradual moral concession leads down a slippery slope. Before you know it, behaviors that would have once seemed unacceptable become normalized through incremental steps. As abuses of power go unchecked, people become desensitized until corruption permeates the entire organizational culture.

But the early stages offer a critical window where intervention can still be effective. Speaking truth to power requires courage in the beginning but prevents downstream devastation. When integrity alarms are sounded, reminding leaders of shared values and the dangers of ethical drift, it gives them a chance to correct course before permanent damage is done.

Early truth-telling maintains cultural guardrails and acts as an immune response to moral threats. For this reason, empowering respectful opposition and having the wisdom to heed those voices helps organizations avoid falling prey to ethical mishaps. But this depends on a foundation of trust and justice. The key is establishing openness early before patterns become deep rooted. Preventing large-scale corruption hinges on addressing small compromises quickly through moral courage in the beginning stages.

Rehabilitating Toxic Cultures

Transforming toxic cultures requires systemic, rigorous interventions:

- Reset expectations through values-driven leadership and aligning policies, processes, and incentives accordingly.
- Increase transparency practices, including open dialogue, town halls, and the protection of whistleblowers.
- Confront denial and demand accountability for past abuses to break corrupt norms.
- Provide diversity and inclusion training to reduce biases.
- Establish community-building practices to proactively repair broken trust.
- Audit and amend aspects of physical workspaces impacting psychological safety.

With sustained commitment to humanistic practices, pockets of integrity widen until reaching critical mass. But superficial reforms merely disguise toxicity temporarily. Leaders must address root causes with moral courage. Here lies the only viable path to cultural rehabilitation - through truth, justice, and people-centered systems nurturing our best selves, not our worst instincts. Though difficult, this journey redeems both leaders and organizations.

Corruption Warnings from History

Examining leadership disasters through history reveals how unchecked toxicity starts:

Enron

The business world reeled after energy giant Enron's massive accounting fraud imploded in 2001. But warning signs of warped cultural values appeared much earlier. Driven by a win-at-all-costs culture, Enron exploited legal loopholes and unprecedented political influence to pursue ever greater profits and prestige. Ruthless internal competition bred unethical practices. Critiquing leadership was taboo.

But behind the scenes, insiders were growing troubled. Accountant Sherron Watkins warned CEO Ken Lay of massive fraud in a now famous memo stating, "We're such a crooked company." But Ken Lay ignored the alarms. Without intervention, Enron's toxic culture eventually collapsed under the weight of its own corruption. Thousands lost jobs and pensions built on deceit. A ship can only sail so far before rotting holes below deck spring forth. There is a detrimental fate of cultures that are more obsessed with image than ethical foundations.

Wells Fargo

In 2016, Wells Fargo's decades of aggressive sales culture erupted in scandal when regulators discovered millions of fraudulent accounts created by employees under pressure. Driven by intense leadership pressure for unrelenting growth, employees resorted to unethical practices to hit sales targets. Whistleblowers who spoke up faced retaliation. This cultural toxicity corroded integrity at every level.

CEO John Stumpf initially downplayed the fraud as isolated instances. But soon, evidence revealed a deep-rooted problem. The warped cultural values he had nurtured pressured people to cheat or be fired. Wells Fargo shows how otherwise ethical individuals compromise morals when pressured by toxic systems. But accountability and reform can yet restore integrity. There is hope if corruption is confronted with courage, not denial.

Volkswagen

In 2015, Volkswagen's gleaming reputation crumbled when engineers were caught installing devices to falsify emissions data. Speed and success had become cultural mandates that overrode ethics. Though shocking, the scandal did not spring from nowhere. Author Bill Vlasic wrote, "The company culture that gave rise to the cheating was the result of an internal competition..." Employees felt intense pressure to build hot cars while meeting strict emissions standards.

Fearing the consequences of failure, engineers resorted to deception. But when the truth emerged, it threatened the company's very survival. Volkswagen offers a sobering case of goal-oriented cultures losing moral perspective. But redemption remains possible through self-reflection and cultural realignment to core values.

Leadership is an honor and a grave responsibility. The fates of civilizations echo the character of kings and councils charged with wise stewardship. But vain tyrants chase self-interest over justice. Therein, we see by negative example the urgent duty of moral leadership - to bend the arc of history toward truth and righteousness.

The Leader's Legacy

Leadership carries immense responsibility because influence is hard-won but easily lost. The cultural seeds that leaders plant will blossom for years to come, for good or ill. Toxic leaders poison organizations and distort norms through fear, deception, and compromised standards. Their dysfunctional modeling grants permission for others to embrace darker human impulses like greed, deceit, and selfishness. Leaders set the tone. As John

C. Maxwell so eloquently states: "Everything rises and falls on leadership."

In contrast, wisdom and integrity produce humanity's better angels. Ethical leaders shape cultures where people rise to meet high expectations with accountability. Their example gives followers the courage to stand up for what is right. Ultimately, every leader's legacy manifests in the morals, behaviors, and performance of the people and organizations left behind. A leader's influence echoes through history long after they depart.

That is why we must each rededicate ourselves regularly to the solemn duties of leadership. The shadows cast by both noble and dysfunctional leaders stretch far. May we each reflect deeply on the seeds we are planting through our influence on culture. Humanity will rise or fall based on the moral quality of leaders. Leadership carries a profound responsibility and privilege. The greatest legacy is to leave behind more moral people equipped to make the world a bit brighter.

Chapter Summary:

- Toxic leaders deliberately manipulate cultural dynamics, normalizing dysfunction until ethical foundations erode. But healthy environments empower resistance to corrosion. Understanding these subtle forces allows intervention before permanent pollution.

- Hypocrisy destroys trust. When leaders exempt themselves from organizational standards, it signals the rules are for lesser members. But integrity aligns words with actions. Moral consistency at the top inspires cultural renewal.

- Hyper-competitive cultures fueled by ruthless leaders sacrifice ethics for results. But collaboration focused on collective growth yields superior outcomes. Functional leaders avoid encouraging harmful behaviors in others.

- Physical spaces substantially impact psychological experiences. Depriving environments breed toxicity. Offices designed with people in mind, that make them feel valued and in control, help them to think creatively and work well together. Careful design of buildings and workspaces can help people reach their full potential.

- A society that only cares about success without considering what is right and wrong will eventually fall apart. However, with accountability, courage, and reform, redemption remains possible by realigning to core values. Leaders shape the future by setting examples of good behavior that others follow for many years.

Chapter 12 | Healing the Dysfunctional Culture

Solutions for Turning Around Unhealthy Organizational Cultures Created by Toxic Leaders

Of all the complex challenges leaders face, few prove more daunting yet rewarding than guiding the rehabilitation of an organization after a period of toxic culture. Transforming dysfunctional group norms requires tremendous perseverance, compassion, and moral courage over an extended time. However, the arduous journey of incremental renewal yields rich rewards as both leaders and team members experience redemption.

In this chapter, we will explore practical strategies to pursue cultural renewal in the aftermath of unethical or abusive leadership. The road ahead remains difficult. Progress will be slow and punctuated by setbacks that test commitment. However, step-by-step, with care, humility and faith in human potential, even the most severely poisoned cultures can be gradually transformed into psychologically healthy and thriving communities.

There is hope for restoration, even amid the devastation. With determined effort, the wounds of toxicity can give way to growth. And broken bonds can become stronger through reconciliation. But real change means committing to the long process of bold, caring leadership. Leaders must ground themselves in understanding that cultural healing is not an event, but an arduous journey. It is a marathon, not a sprint. By internalizing this, they gain patience and perspective to sustain the taxing work of renewal even when progress seems uncertain.

For in the end, an organization's culture manifests through its people - their morals, relationships, and collective purpose. And people inherently seek connection, meaning, and goodness. By tapping into these core human needs, authentic cultural transformation remains possible in time.

Therein lies the deepest source of motivation along the long road ahead. May we proceed with realistic hope, moral purpose, and care for one another. And may we plant seeds each day through courageous leadership that will blossom into cultural fruits we may not live to see, but that sustain those to come. The destination makes the difficult journey worth embracing together.

Cut Off the Head: Removing Toxic Leaders

There once was a prestigious university whose president was uncovered harassing employees. Despite public outrage, the board was reluctant to terminate his prestigious tenure. But the dysfunction continued festering. It was only after an ultimatum from major donors that the president was finally removed. Immediately, the campus climate began improving.

When advanced toxicity takes root, surgical leadership removal becomes essential so recovery can begin. Deranged influence must be severed to halt further damage. But self-preservation instincts make rotten leaders fiercely resistant to relinquishing power. External pressure from vocal stakeholders often proves critical.

If termination is unattainable, isolating and restricting their authority can limit damage. Oversight systems must provide checks and balances beyond their control. But understand that these remain temporary band-aids, not cures. As Lao Tzu wrote, "To lead people, walk behind them." Toxic leaders who refuse to walk behind must be left behind for cultural healing to begin. A kingdom cannot flourish when tyrants yet rule from the shadows. Casting them out into the light offers the only path forward.

Transparency and Accountability: Creating Openness

Toxic cultures breed freely in the darkness. To begin disinfecting corrupted behaviors, leaders must throw open shuttered windows and allow the light of transparency to expose dysfunction. Healing and justice require openness, however uncomfortable for those enduring it. Key transparency measures include:

- Protecting whistleblowers - They are antibodies within the organization exposing misconduct.
- Conducting open town halls - Empower all voices to be heard, especially marginalized ones.
- Establishing anonymous feedback channels - Removing barriers to free information flow.
- Sending cultural pulse surveys - Diagnosing issues through unfiltered data.
- Appointing external oversight committees - Independent third-party perspectives counter false assumptions.
- Auditing and reforming policies - Aligning formal rules with adopted values, closing trust gaps.

- Releasing records and data openly - Sunlight motivates self-correction.

While transparency risks revealing unpleasant realities, authentic healing only occurs through openness, however painful. As Martin Luther King wrote, "Darkness cannot drive out darkness; only light can do that." Therefore, leaders must take bold action if there is any hope left of redeeming the organizational culture. The dark truths must be brought to light before the light can return.

Rewriting the Rules: Aligning Policies with Values

An organization's formal processes and incentive structures represent cultural cornerstones that shape behaviors. But when these concrete policies, procedures, and reward systems conflict with adopted values, they actively undermine the stated principles leaders profess. All too often, leaders issue lofty clichés about integrity, teamwork, accountability, and other noble values. Yet they leave underlying misaligned rules and frameworks intact that breed toxicity and counterproductive conduct. To truly transform toxic cultures plagued by "say-do" gaps, courageous leaders must undertake the exhausting but essential work of rigorously evaluating existing operational models for consistency with principles. This includes:

- Comprehensively auditing and reviewing all formal policies, procedures, guidelines, and handbooks against stated cultural values and ethics to identify inconsistencies. Excuses for inconsistencies can't be accepted.
- Eliminating unnecessary, outdated, or cumbersome procedures that inadvertently promote unethical behavior,

moral disconnection, harmful workarounds, or other toxic outcomes.

- Instituting carefully designed incentives, recognition programs, performance metrics, and reward structures that tangibly promote and reinforce desired cultural behaviors. Ineffective incentives must be abolished.

- Auditing current power structures, decision rights, and the distribution of authority across leadership levels to discern imbalances, bottle necks, and "shadow rules" that undercut adopted values.

- Increasing legitimate bottom-up participation in decision making through empowered teams, grassroots innovation channels, and other forms of employee feedback.

- Mandatory checkpoints for ethical considerations and alignment with values should be added in all planning and governance processes.

While immensely exhausting, this comprehensive examination provides a pivotal opportunity to finally align the adopted values leaders want with the tangible policies, procedures, structures, and incentives that actually govern daily behaviors. This exhaustive work provides the opportunity to ignite an authentic cultural renewal grounded in shared values across every part of the organization. But superficial reforms will merely breed skepticism and distrust. Leaders must demonstrate the courage to fundamentally rewrite underlying rules and social codes. This will be the only viable path forward to institute lasting ethical transformations versus lip service.

Restoring Trust: Rebuilding Relationships and Morale

Organizational culture ultimately lies in the collective space between people. To truly heal toxic cultures, leaders must focus on repairing the broken interpersonal connections, communication channels, and bonds of trust that exist within the organization. This undertaking requires implementing shared renewal processes and rituals that aim to rebuild relationships fractured by prior toxic periods or unethical leadership. Some examples include:

- Establishing truth and reconciliation platforms for people to acknowledge past interpersonal harms and offer sincere apologies, forgiveness, and pledges to do better. The goal is reflection, growth, and establishing mutual understanding.
- Providing extensive coaching, mediation, and conflict resolution programs to compassionately address festering conflicts between individuals, clarify misunderstandings, and strengthen fragmented bonds.
- Conducting thorough trainings on psychological safety, diversity, healthy communication, and emotional intelligence to foster overall interpersonal trust, perspective-taking, and empathy.
- Holding team building activities focused on forging shared goals, collaborative spirit, and camaraderie to short-circuit unproductive competition.
- Designing corrective emotional experiences through habits of care and moral elevation to help replace past relational trauma and distrust with positive associations.

- Implementing peer-to-peer gratitude practices, recognition, and appreciation processes to tangibly reinforce people's value and contributions, countering past neglect.

- Encouraging organization-wide self-care, sabbaticals, resilience training, and work-life balance to prevent employee burnout that can corrode cultural bonds.

- While demanding, these communal healing measures aim to incrementally rebuild broken human connections and relationships following periods of severe dysfunction or unethical leadership. However, it remains essential that leaders not just facilitate such cultural healing processes but also actively participate alongside employees. They must model desired behaviors authentically. This represents the only viable way to rebuild broken interpersonal trust and gradually start an ethical, cultural renewal.

The Leader's Journey: From Toxic to Transformative

In studying dysfunctional leaders, a predictable trajectory often emerges - skills without judgment inflate selfish pride, and not care for others. Talents meant to serve others get highjacked toward selfish goals. But this descent into toxicity typically results from a leader losing perspective, not innate character flaws. Even the most detached and dysfunctional leaders were once well-intentioned. They simply wandered far down misleading paths, increasingly unable to find their way back alone. But redemption remains possible when leaders courageously confront their shadows and reorient towards the light.

As Paulo Coelho wrote, "The darkest hour has only 60 minutes." The key is rediscovering one's inner moral compass before it becomes buried too deeply under layers of dysfunctional behavior and toxicity. With rigorous self-reflection and redemptive guidance, even leaders who have lost their way for seasons need not remain perpetually lost.

This is the simple advice I offer after decades of being a student of leadership. The capability to lead well and do good remains within us all, often just buried temporarily. But by daring to walk in the light with wisdom, integrity, and care for people, we regain hope and direction from even the darkest valleys.

May we each rediscover and reconnect to the essential virtues that make leadership worthy of one's entire life. The trajectory of every leader contains ups and downs. But who we become through the journey defines our destination. And there is always time to change course.

Chapter Summary:

- Transforming toxic cultures is a marathon requiring tremendous perseverance, compassion, and moral courage over the years. But gradually, both leaders and organizations experience renewal by rediscovering humanity.
- Severing dysfunctional influence through removal or restrictions halts further cultural damage. But authentic healing requires deeper systemic change. Letting light in through transparency and accountability reforms broken systems and assumptions.
- Beyond policies, cultural renewal repairs damaged connections between people. Renewal rites like reconciliation, conflict resolution and team building

gradually rebuild trust. Leaders must exemplify desired behaviors alongside staff.

- Toxic dysfunction often results from losing moral perspective, not natural evil. With self-reflection and support, misguided leaders can rediscover their inner compass. Their descent into shadows need not be permanent. There is always hope in the light.

- Growth begins by taking responsibility for the pain caused then walking with humility towards restoration. By modeling service over ego, humbled leaders regain influence. And by lifting others up from darkness, they rise together. Therein lies the path from toxic to transformative.

Chapter 13 | The Cost of Being a Functional Leader

While the rewards of positively influencing others remain immeasurable, embracing functional leadership also carries heavy consequences we must soberly count. Profound sacrifices and trials await those who take up the mantle. Before accepting the call to lead, we must reflect solemnly with eyes wide open to the immense burden upon our backs. We must steel our minds, hearts, and wills to weather the harsh realities ahead.

In this chapter, I share cautions forged through difficult experiences I did not fully appreciate as a young leader. Leading well extracts realities far beyond the imagination of the untested. Our courage will face intense fire. Those unprepared for the furnace ahead will inevitably crack.

But by staring unflinchingly at leadership's greatest challenges, we gain perspective to understand the proving ahead. Hardship should never deter us from leading boldly. But neither can we afford to underestimate the incredible selflessness required to lead with integrity over the long term. The path of being a functional leader is noble, but narrow. Sacrifices await around each turn. Before committing yourself for the long haul, ponder deeply. And prepare to pay prices far steeper than most fathom. But know that fulfillment awaits those willing to rise to leadership's highest callings.

You Will Make Hard Decisions Affecting People You Care About

Leaders must often make excruciating choices that negatively impact people, even loyal team members giving their utmost. Leadership brings the heavy burden of decisions that influence lives. Navigating complex trade-offs between business realities and human needs falls on leaders' shoulders alone. Though guided by values, leaders themselves draw the lines determining where burdens get allocated.

Leaders will inevitably miscalculate, wound others unintentionally, or delay responding when urgency calls for swift action. Such failures bruise one's spirit. But all leaders will make imperfect decisions that bring pain to someone, somewhere. Many cannot stomach the anguish that accompanies such difficult decision-making. But meaning emerges in pursuing purposes greater than oneself. Leadership is not for the faint of heart. It requires sacrificing personal comfort for the greater good.

Before accepting the mantle of leadership, assess honestly if status or acclaim motivates more than agony over consequences. Leadership demands diminishing ego to serve others. Significant internal storms await those who guide any flock. It is in these difficult moments of sacrifice that the deeper moral purpose of leadership emerges.

You Will Be Disliked Despite Your Good Intentions

Leadership inevitably attracts criticism, even when intentions are noble, and actions aim to advance the collective good. Most decisions result in loud criticism and disagreement. By nature, leadership requires taking a stand on complex issues with no perfect solutions. Despite striving to serve justly, some branded leaders' imperfect choices as conspiracies or evil.

Influence attracts scrutiny. The higher leaders ascend, the more critics emerge to throw stones. All leaders face envy and public misperceptions of their true intentions. Leaders must stand firm on principles, not popularity. The conviction to follow their moral compass despite disapproval separates great leaders from the rest. Leadership requires weathering personal attacks to achieve lasting change. No crown fully secures itself. Leadership legacies hang on courageously, upholding values that weigh more than immediate approval. Criticism tests, butdoes not break principled leaders anchored in higher purposes.

You Will Be Misunderstood Without the Ability to Defend Yourself

Leaders inevitably get misunderstood and misjudged, with limited ability to defend themselves. By nature of their public position, leaders receive heavy scrutiny. Leaders live in glass houses and are prone to misinterpretation. Critics hijack attention while functional leaders silently focus on duties. False assumptions thrive. Influential leaders lose privacy and control over narratives shaping their reputations. Trying to defend themselves often worsens perceptions when scrutiny peaks.

In my career as a pastor, I sometimes had to make difficult decisions based on private information that I could not share publicly. I could not reveal confidential details, even though it meant people did not understand my full reasoning. This was challenging because I wanted to justify my choices but could not disclose sensitive information that might hurt others. As a leader,

I had to accept that I would be misunderstood rather than violate confidence, even when it meant facing criticism.

Unfair misjudgments can damage leaders' reputations instantly, with restoration taking years. Attempting public defense risks amplifying criticism rather than dispelling it. At times, leaders have little recourse but to endure injustice patiently. Their true character and motivations remain apparent only to their conscience and loved ones. Nonetheless, with time, the full context and complexities in leaders' stories typically emerge. Their complete leadership legacies, encompassing lifetimes of service, speak for themselves.

Weathering misjudgment challenges leaders to exemplify grace under fire. Despite wounds, they must model poise and restraint. But an honorable focus on worthy service makes vicious words ring hollow over time. Leaders will face periods when reputation hinges on factors beyond their control. However, staying dedicated to their purpose helps leaders rise above temporary criticism. All leaders face some scorn, but history ultimately evaluates their leadership accurately.

You Will Have Difficult Conversations That Will Ultimately Bring Improvement

Leaders must hold difficult conversations to improve their organizations. Whether confronting poor performance, unethical actions, interpersonal conflicts or other dysfunctional dynamics, these tough discussions cause short-term discomfort but drive long-term gains. Skirting candid dialogue allows problems to fester. But leaders who lead courageous conversations create change. They give voice to unspoken truths that others avoid surfacing. These exchanges foster understanding, accountability, and solutions to recurring issues.

Approaching difficult dialogues requires emotional intelligence, empathy, and care. Leaders must balance truth with support. Their goal is illuminating realities to spur improvement, not attacking the individual. Dialogue should center on specific behaviors or incidents, not character assassinations. It often helps to assume good intent--that the other person likely does not realize the negative impacts of their actions. Explain the situation objectively and ask for their perspective. Find common ground and reinforce shared goals.

The most effective leaders have difficult conversations early before problems escalate. They create psychologically safe environments where people know the discussion is meant to help, not harm them. However, these tough conversations usually involve some uncomfortable moments before reaching a shared understanding. Discomfort signifies you are presenting critical issues. Leaders capable of pushing past initial tensions to alignment gain immense influence. Have the courage to drive the conversations needed to guide teams forward. Progress emerges from care, candor, and listening.

Sharpening the Saw Through Intentional Leadership

As part of my semi-annual practice, I held dedicated one-on-one sessions with each team member. These sessions created a safe space for open and non-judgmental dialogues about all aspects of their work experience. It resembled an informal performance review but focused on their holistic wellbeing. I established a safe environment for them to express concerns without fear of reprimand or retaliation. My role was to listen intently and ask probing questions to understand their realities.

This practice draws inspiration from the parable of two lumberjacks competitively chopping down trees. One periodically stopped to sharpen his saw while the other chopped relentlessly with his dull blade until exhausted. By pausing to "sharpen the saw," we emerge re-energized and more effective. Similarly, these sessions offered my team an opportunity to "sharpen" themselves by sharing anything on their minds - professional or personal. They appreciated the emotional outlet. In return, I gained invaluable insights into motivating and supporting my team.

Often, in leadership, we get so absorbed in day-to-day operations that we neglect our team's holistic health. But wisdom knows that consistently "sharpening the saw" empowers teams to chop stronger when it matters most. By creating space for open dialogue and rejuvenation, leaders invest in the long-term flourishing of people. A dull axe quickly loses cutting power. But consistent maintenance keeps tools - and teams - functioning at their best.

You Will Hold People Accountable When They Fail or Act Unethically

Leaders must hold team members accountable when they fail to meet expectations or act unethically. Accountability is key to maintaining high standards. Addressing poor performance requires candidly giving concrete feedback focused on behaviors, not character. Set clear expectations. Offer support to improve. But also establish consequences for continued issues.

When misconduct occurs, act swiftly. Document infractions thoroughly. Confront problems head on while assuming positive intent. Hear people out and identify root causes. But also enforce consistent policies. Exercise wisdom in giving discipline. The goal is correcting behaviors, not punishment. Consider contextual factors and mitigating circumstances. But avoid double standards for certain individuals.

Unethical actions demand direct intervention. Clarify the misconduct, its impact and expectations going forward. Impose fair consequences aligned to policies. Provide opportunities for restitution when possible. Severing ties should be a last resort when other efforts to correct behavior fail. However, toxic individuals unwilling to change must be removed to protect culture.

Holding people accountable is difficult but necessary. It maintains standards, provides clarity, and gives people an opportunity to improve. Delaying accountability enables problems to grow. Functional leaders address issues promptly and directly. No one enjoys receiving corrections. But consistent accountability builds trust and respect. It shows leaders are invested in the team's collective success. Ensure accountability with compassion but conviction.

You Will Share Credit Rather Than Taking all the Glory

Functional leaders share credit and give others recognition rather than taking all the glory for themselves. Uplifting teams requires spotlighting the contributions of team members. Praise excellent work publicly. Acknowledge achievements in team meetings or organizational platforms. Recognition deepens engagement and motivates top performance. Celebrate the contributions of all team members, not just stars. Every role advances collective goals. Take time to understand each person's impact. Then, tailor appreciation specific to their efforts. Model humility by spotlighting others rather than yourself. Credit teams for successes. Thank individuals who played key assists. Set the tone by showcasing achievement at all levels. Share recognition with managers of high achievers. Praising managers supports further employee development. It also models collaborative leadership for them to copy.

Selfless leaders build cultures of appreciation where everyone feels valued. They focus praise on people who dislike public attention. Quiet achievers are often overlooked and thus most deserving of external validation. Avoid excessive self-promotion. Seek only to elevate your team and organization. People resent leaders who hog the credit. But they deeply respect leaders who share the stage. Uplift others and downplay your own role. Leadership means putting the team above oneself. Prioritize opportunities for team members to gain visibility and build careers. Lead so no one realizes you are there.

You Will Be Pressured to Compromise Your Values

Leaders inevitably face pressure to compromise their values. External forces and moral dilemmas will test leaders' principles. But compromising integrity for expediency damages credibility and trust. As scrutiny and stakes heighten, the pull intensifies to cut ethical corners. Some will peddle rationalizations that unethical actions serve the greater good. But leaders grounded in moral clarity resist corroding forces.

Establish safeguards to filter out voices lacking integrity. Consult advisors with strong values to maintain perspective.

Revisit core purpose and principles before key decisions. When facing gray area dilemmas, aim higher than minimum standards. Error on the side of transparency and caution. Question anything promoting self-interest over stakeholders. Upholding ethical culture requires disciplined consistency. Leaders face temptation when their ambitious plans face setbacks or delays. In desperation to force outcomes, principles can blur. But moving fast matters less than moving ethically. Patience and perseverance honor values under pressure.

Finally, skeptics will perpetually question the motives of principled leaders. But focus on aligning words and deeds. Let conduct speak for itself. Those grounded in humility and purpose can withstand the fiery trials of principle that the insincere cannot. Stay centered in the knowledge that success devoid of ethics and human decency rings hollow. Compromising values sacrifices meaning for short-term gain. However, leadership is truly worth committing to, and it stands firm on internal truth even amid external pressure.

You Will Make Personal Sacrifices for Others

Leadership requires making tremendous personal sacrifices for the greater good. Long hours can make weekends normal. Leaders can sacrifice health, comfort, and relationships to fulfill their calling. Family life can often suffer the deepest. Spouses feel the absence of attention. Children seldom understand why a parent's focus pulls elsewhere. Leaders can support loved ones financially but still deprive them emotionally.

Sacrifices accumulate until burnout becomes common. The same dedication that fuels effective leadership can exhaust them over time. Self-care becomes even more essential. Yet service calls, especially during crises, cannot be delegated. True leaders feel compelled to be the first to make sacrifices and the last to demand fair burdens in return. They forgo privileges that could be claimed.

This selflessness earns immense respect. Followers will imitate the sacrifice modeled by leaders who give of themselves without expectation of reciprocation. But martyr mentalities should be avoided. There are always more battles; pace yourself for the long haul. Still, leadership means absorbing pains, so others feel them less severely. Wise leaders find meaning in securing a better future, even if they will not fully experience it themselves. Fulfillment comes from planting seeds and equipping the next generation.

Leaders must remember that no matter how heavy their load, it pales beside the sacrifices of those they serve. Stay grounded by spending time among people your work impacts. Their progress fuels your purpose. True leadership means giving all of yourself so that others may live fuller lives. The fulfilment of knowing your sacrifices uplifted others makes the costs worthwhile.

You Will Experience the Loneliness That Accompanies Authority

Leaders can often experience the profound loneliness that accompanies positions of authority. The higher leaders rise, the more alone they become. This isolation is an inherent burden of leadership. Few truly understand the pressures faced at the top. Confiding with subordinates about personal struggles feel inappropriate. Peers become competitors, not companions. Even family cannot fully relate to leadership challenges.

Meanwhile, everyone seeks answers and assurance from the leader. But leaders have nowhere to turn when they themselves need counsel. Their circle shrinks as all look to them for wisdom and strength. Leaders also get isolated through controversy and unpopularity. Attacks can originate externally and internally. But leaders must stand alone on principle when challenged. This loneliness of command further separates them.

Authority itself distances leaders from others. Subordinates behave cautiously around the boss. Friendships change. Being "on stage" means constantly filtering words and actions, depriving leaders of intimacy that requires vulnerability. Leadership transitions bring especially acute loneliness. Letting go of old identities means shedding former support systems. But it takes time to build trust in new roles. Seasons of solitude should be expected.

The burdens of leadership are supposed to be borne alone. But isolation need not mean desolation. Wise leaders proactively develop outlets, confidants, and communities to nurture their humanity. They remember that leadership is not an identity; it is merely a temporary role to fulfill. Priorities that give leadership meaning – faith, family, friends, and service – sustain them until it passes.

You Will Need to Model Strength in Crises

Leaders must model strength and stability when crises strike. In difficult times, people look to the leader for reassurance and resolve. Their courage under fire sets the tone. Show calm determination over panic. Speak with measured confidence. Avoid knee-jerk reactions in favor of thoughtful deliberation.

Your discipline instills calm. Succumbing to fear breeds wider anxiety.

Share information transparently. Admit what you do not know. But reaffirm your commitment to navigating through uncertainty together. Your raw authenticity builds solidarity and resilience. Do not minimize crises but put them in proper perspective. Context reduces alarm. Remind people of prior challenges overcome through cooperation. Their faith will grow through your steadiness.

Uplift others through encouragement and expressions of confidence. Focus their eyes on higher purposes being served, even amid trials. Great leaders transform fear into moral power. They know hope impels action. Attend first to the human needs of those affected. Provide practical relief and comfort before addressing logistical details. Show caring, which kindles courage and sacrifice. Model personal sacrifice by working tirelessly and forfeiting privileges. But also monitor your stress levels. Burnout impairs the sound judgment required most in turmoil. Prioritize health to serve long-term.

Leaders should expect piercing scrutiny during crises. But stay focused on solutions over appearances. Criticism fades, but your conduct remains an example for others. Lead through the storm with purpose. Endure the heaviness that comes with responsibility. But find strength in those your leadership serves. Their progress makes the burden bearable. Lead so they may endure and thrive beyond the crisis.

You Will Be Targeted by Those Threatened By Change

Leaders driving change inevitably get targeted by those who feel threatened by it. Vested interests and gatekeepers push back hard to preserve power and old ways. Opposition is fiercest when reforms challenge deeply entrenched norms, power structures and inefficient processes. Even positive changes disrupt comfortable status quo. Many people benefit from broken systems and resist improvements. Resistance often turns personal against change leaders. They get vilified as radical, idealistic, or incompetent. Personal attacks aim to damage credibility and isolate them.

Effective leaders anticipate and prepare for backlash. They steady themselves against malicious rumors and criticism. Building a broad coalition of diverse supporters provides cover and moral courage when pressure intensifies. Change agents must distinguish valid critiques from blind attacks. Some resistance raises important concerns about change rollout and unintended consequences. Leaders should solicit feedback humbly rather than dismissing all critics. However, they must also recognize when opposition stems from deep-rooted prejudices or fear of loss. Old mentalities will not change through reason but through the demonstration of new paradigm shifts. Leaders press forward backed by conviction.

Finally, not all resistors can be won over. Some become outright obstructionists. Leaders must have the courage to evaluate when opposition has become toxic rather than thoughtful. Relentless sabotage may require changes in personnel. Leading change requires resilience, coalition-building and unwavering conviction. Attacks hurt most when intentions are noble. But leaders must rise above the fray to serve the greater good. Endure harsh words; avoid harsh responses. In time, as the old gives way to the new, progress speaks for itself.

You Will Lead Others Who May One Day Replace You Rather Than Reward You

Leaders often develop others who may one day replace them rather than reward them. But this reality captures true leadership. Great leaders focus on empowering successors rather than preserving their own power. Identify emerging talent even if it threatens your position. Mentor others unselfishly. Let go of insecurities; avoid viewing developing leaders as competitors. Instead, take pride in raising new generations who are equipped to advance the mission. Jesus embodied this mindset when he stated in John 14:12 that those who follow him would do even greater things than he had done. The greatest leaders seek to empower others to reach heights that exceed their own achievements.

Model servant leadership by pouring into those following you. Guide them towards growth opportunities you wish you had. Use your experience and relationships to open doors for their careers or callings. Willingly give up attention and credit as the leaders you develop gain increasing prominence and authority. Embrace moments when their light shines brighter than yours. Gradually hand over authority as they demonstrate readiness.

Leadership is not forever. We are tenants entrusted for a season to steward those rising behind us. Even the highest thrones will sit empty when we depart. Our lives are but single links in longer chains. Accept that your greatest legacy is embodied in others' increased capacity. Your lasting influence flows through those you empowered. Even your own displacement by a worthy successor represents the ultimate fulfillment of leadership. The heavens celebrate when leaders accomplish their purpose of rendering themselves obsolete by empowering others to soar. Such selfless leadership multiplies influence down generations. Fearlessly develop your replacement--it means your work endures. Help many stand tall once you depart off the scene.

Leading Functionally Requires Principles Above Popularity

Leading with integrity requires prioritizing principles over pursuing popularity. Functional leadership serves purposes beyond amassing power or praise. Leaders must live and lead by timeless values - not fickle opinions. Many love influencing others but shrink from the sacrifices authentic leadership demands. They crave attention over accountability. This confuses celebrity with leadership. True leaders stand for truth when it costs them support. They accept criticism as the price of conviction. Public opinion ebbs and flows, but principles remain steady landmarks that direct the way. Lead for those who will inherit the future, not just present critics. Withstand fiery trials of commitment. Focus on empowering those you serve over tallying personal achievements. Pursue justice and innovation even amid resistance.

True leadership requires leading by your moral principles, even if it means standing alone against the tide of popular opinion. But conviction provides sturdy ballast through storms of scorn. Making sacrifices for your principles earns genuine, lasting respect - more than the fleeting fame given to those chasing trends.

Simplify decision processes by filtering out considerations of personal popularity or self-interest. Leaders get bogged down when they consider anything other than the right moral choice.

Focusing solely on principles provides clarity that allows leaders to act decisively and confidently. The fulfilled life invests fully in purposes greater than the self. Leadership worthy of that life holds fast to the truth when pressure mounts. Keep your anchor buried deep in time-tested principles. All else will pass away-- only integrity remains.

Chapter Summary:

- Leadership carries immense burdens most underestimate - agony over imperfect decisions affecting others, criticism despite good intentions, and misjudgment without recourse. But meaning emerges in moral purpose and standing on conviction when comfort calls to compromise.

- Candid conversations produce progress but short-term discomfort. Still, leaders must speak hard truths with care. Sharpening team strength requires creating space for renewal and mutually uplifting growth. Accountability and integrity cannot be avoided but demand compassion.

- Loneliness accompanies influence as circles shrink. But selflessness earns immense respect - putting team first, equipping successors to advance the mission. Leadership uplifts communities, not feeding ego. Stand on time-tested principles above popularity that passes.

- Change agents invariably get targeted amid reform but must press on. Endure criticism through coalition-building and resilience, avoiding harsh responses. Rebuke may hurt, but conviction provides ballast in storms. Stay fixed on purpose greater than self - therein lies fulfillment.

- Crisis exposes mettle but also hones it for those lending others strength. Backlash tests patience and questions fitness but only purifies perseverance. Leadership develops through trials. The path narrows uphill but reaches horizons otherwise missed below. Hardship bears rewards unseen at the outset when embraced as growth.